SADDLE
SERENADERS

# SADDLE SERENADERS

GUY LOGSDON, MARY ROGERS, AND WILLIAM JACOBSON

GIBBS·SMITH
PUBLISHER

SALT LAKE CITY

First Edition
97 96 95   5 4 3 2 1

This is a Peregrine Smith Book, published by
Gibbs Smith, Publisher
P.O. Box 667
Layton, Utah  84041

Design by J. Scott Knudsen, Park City, Utah
Edited by Gail Yngve

Printed and bound in Hong Kong

**Library of Congress Cataloging-in-Publication Data**
Logsdon, Guy William.
Saddle Serenaders / Guy Logsdon, Mary Rogers, William Jacobson.
p. cm.
Includes index.
ISBN 0-87905-604-5
1. Country musicians—United States—Biography. I. Rogers, Mary,
1957-  . II. Jacobson, William, 1957-  . III. Title.
ML394.L64  1995
781.642'092'273—dc20
[B]                                95-1776
                                      CIP
                                      MN

*This book is dedicated to all
cowboy and western music lovers who
have truly kept this music alive.*

The Authors

"It's mighty encouraging to see the interest in
the cowboy and West phenomenon continue to
grow. I just hope it doesn't become too big
because that's when the corporate weasels turn
into homogenized fodder for the sterile
digestive tracts of the mindless mainstream."

Don Edwards

# ACKNOWLEDGMENTS

The idea for this book came from Gibbs Smith, and we thank him for his support of western music and musicians. Madge Baird and Gail Yngve suffered long months of coaxing overdue manuscript and illustrations from us; we extend our appreciation to them for their patience and understanding and hard work. We are indebted to the musicians who took the time to respond to our request for personal information, and we thank each one of you.

For information about deceased musicians and about cowboy and western music, we turned to many sources. Scholars, collectors, and fans have researched and documented numerous individuals who contributed to our western culture, and if we have failed to acknowledge any of these writers, we want you to know that it was an oversight, not deliberate.

The journals *Song of the West, JEMF Quarterly, Old Time Music, The Journal of Country Music,* and *Record Research* provided invaluable information as did liner notes for long play records, most of which are now collectors' items.

We turned to the works of Ken Griffis, Norm Cohen, Archie Green, Bill Malone, Judith McCulloh, John I. White, Ronnie Pugh, Cary Ginell, Glen White, Brian Rust, Doug Green, William Koon, Carol Collins, Bob Pinson, Bob Healy, Tony Russell, Rich Kienzle, Charles Wolfe, Fred G. Hoeptner, Charles Townsend, Jim Bob Tinsley, Stanley Kilarr, Mark Humphrey, and many, many more. Additional thanks for their valuable contributions: Bridget Dolan, Michael Gross, Vincent Lara, O. J. Sikes, David Skepner, Kathy Lynn Wills, and Howard E. Wright.

The following books were reference sources: Bill C. Malone, *Country Music U.S.A.*, revised and enlarged edition (Austin: University of Texas Press, 1985); John I. White, *Git Along, Little Dogies* (Urbana: University of Illinois Press, 1975); Fred Dollar and Roy Thompson, *The Illustrated Encyclopedia of Country Music* (New York: Harmony Books, 1977); Melvin Shestack, *The Country Music Encyclopedia* (New York: Thomas Y. Crowell Co., 1974); Irwin Stambaler and Grelun Landon, *Encyclopedia of Folk, Country and Western Music* (New York: St. Martin's Press, 1969); Ken Griffis, *Hear My Song, The Story of the Celebrated Sons of the Pioneers* (Camarillo: Norken, revised edition, 1986); Roy Rogers, Dale Evans with Carlton Stowers, *Happy Trails* (New York: Guideposts, 1979); Country Joe Flint and Judy Nelson, *The Insider's Country Music Handbook* (Salt Lake City: Gibbs Smith, Publisher, 1993); Arthur F. McClure and Ken D. Jones, *Heroes, Heavies, and Sagebrush* (New York: A. S. Barnes and Company, 1972); and David Rothel, *The Singing Cowboys* (New York: A. S. Barnes and Company, 1978).

Discographical information came from Guthrie T. Meade's unpublished *Discography of Traditional Songs* and *Tunes on Hillbilly Records* in the Library of Congress, American Folklife Center, Archive of Folk Culture, Washington, D.C.; we express our appreciation to Joseph Hickerson, Gerald Parsons, and staff members in the Archive of Folk Culture.

# INTRODUCTION

*Guy Logsdon*

**"Cheyenne," 1906, is generally considered to be the first Tin Pan Alley western song to be published. (Guy Logsdon and the Ranch House Library.)**

Throughout the recorded history of civilization, each society has had a mythical hero, because a hero unifies a society, particularly when that society is troubled. The American cowboy is our national hero, and every time our society loses faith in itself, interest in the mythical cowboy rises. Cowboy films, music, and radio shows enjoyed an all-time high in popularity during the 1930s. In the 1990s, we see a renewed romance with cowboy culture, specifically with the Oklahoma Cherokee cowboy humorist, Will Rogers, and in cowboy music and poetry.

The working cowboy and the wide-open spaces of the American West captured worldwide creative imagination over a century ago. An infatuation with the free-spirited, independent-minded, and fiercely loyal cowboy blossomed into a romance between the imagined and the real, between the observer and the practitioner. This romance became such a reality that the cowboy became a believer of his own romantic image; this mixed romance created our mythical cowboy.

From this popular mythical conception came an assumption that all cowboys sang songs—songs about their lives, experiences, and beliefs. While there were a few folk songs that used a cowboy theme, and even though a few working cowboys did and do sing, most of the popular cowboy/western songs and singers came, and come, from outside the ranks of working cowboys.

In the twentieth century, radio, phonograph recordings, motion pictures, television, Tin Pan Alley, and even Broadway plays not only strengthened the singing cowboy image, but also contributed to the ever-growing large body of cowboy/western songs. This profusely illustrated book provides biographical information about past and present singers, songwriters, bandleaders, and others involved in cowboy, western, and western swing music. It fills a void created by country music historians who have ignored the importance and contributions of music and musicians west of the Mississippi River.

Country music presently enjoys worldwide popularity, when just a few decades ago it was called "hillbilly" music and was limited to a regional audience. Western music included cowboy songs, string band ballroom dance music, and some hillbilly sounds. It also was limited in appeal, but gained a decade of widespread popularity, particularly in the 1930s, through the movies and recordings of Gene Autry, Roy Rogers, and other saddle serenaders. In the 1940s and 1950s, the two musical forms merged into country/western and slowly became "country."

The western portion was forgotten, but it was music recorded in the West that became crossover music; Gene Autry, Roy Rogers, Bob Wills, and other western artists were not limited to a regional sound or songs. They sang, played, recorded, and broadcast songs and tunes from a wide spectrum—traditional, popular, songs written by or for them, and occasionally songs and tunes from classical music. But even before the aforementioned musicians played and sang crossover tunes, Vernon Dalhart (pseudonym), a Texas singer, was doing it; yet, he has been denied his rightful place as the original popularizer of country/western music. He was a westerner who knew how to sing.

In the 1920s and 1930s, the recording industry set up their equipment regionally, but in the 1940s, the industry had stabilized, and transportation made it easier to have permanent recording studios in a few locations. Los Angeles (Hollywood) became the primary recording center for western music and for some singers/musicians now considered to be country. The sound was distinctively western.

In the 1950s, with television changing the entertainment habits and interests of the nation, country/western slowly moved to Nashville, where it became "country" music. "Western" was removed from the sound until the 1970s, when Johnny Gimble became the "sought after" session fiddler. He returned the western swing sound to country music, and country music's popularity, once again, moved out of regional popularity into worldwide popularity.

"Let 'Er Go" by Will Wood was published in 1907. (Guy Logsdon and the Ranch House Library.)

"My Cowboy Lady" is an example of Tin Pan Alley interest published in 1907 about a cow woman sung by a female. (Guy Logsdon and the Ranch House Library.)

We trust that the following biographies and essays will highlight careers and events that were major contributions to our mythical singing cowboy hero and to the popularity of country music, music that still should be known as country/western. And we apologize for not having entries for Singing Sam Agins, Shelly Lee Alley & His Alley Cats, Jesse Ashlock, The Baker Brothers, Curt Barrett and the Trailsmen Western Dance Band, The Bar-X Cowboys, Paul Bigsby, Cass County Boys, The Chambers, Cindy Church, Bing Crosby, Ivan Daines, Gene Davenport, Denver Darling and His Texas Cowhands, Tex Dean and the Carefree Cowboys, Dolores and the Bluebonnet Boys, Tommy Dover and His Texas Rhythm Boys, Bob Dunn's Vagabonds, Tommy Duren and the Westernaires, Leo Fender, Johnny Gimble, Lou Graham and the Saddlemen, Great Western Orchestra, Tex Grimsley and His Texas Showboys, R. W. Hampton, Leaford Hall and His Texas Vagabonds, Claudie Ham and His Radio Playboys, Slim Harbert & His Boys, Tish Hinojosa, Roy Hogsed and His Rainbow Riders, Charles Huff ("Oklahoma's Own Cowboy Singer") & His Sons of the Plains, Buddy Jones, Margaret Larkin, Benny Leaders with Western Rangers, Dickie McBride & His Village Boys, Mary McCaslin, Walt McCoy and His Western Wonders, Montana Blue, Morris Mills and the Rithumakers (sic), Modern Mountaineers, Johnnie Nelms and the Sunset Cowboys, Roy Newman & His Boys, The Oklahoma Wranglers (Guy, Vic, and Skeeter Willis), Gene O'Quinn with Al Turner's Big "D" Jamboree Barn Dance Gang, Lynn Riggs, Kenny Roberts, Jesse Rodgers, Seven Rowe Brothers Western Swing Band, Ina Sires, Ernie Sites, Bob Skyles and His Skyrockets, Lou Stebner, Ocie Stockard & His Wanderers, The Sunshine Boys, Texas Tophands, Timothy P and Rural Route Three, The Tune Wranglers, Johnny Tyler & His Riders of the Rio Grande, Barney Vardeman and His Drifting Texans, Washtub Jerry, Marc "The Cowboy Crooner" Williams, Foy Willing and Riders of the Purple Sage, Smokey Wood & His Wood Chips, Boots Woodall and the Wranglers, and the hundreds of other cowboy/western singers and musicians who kept the musical tradition alive and popular in the West. If you have information about these people or others we have missed, please send it to Guy Logsdon, 4645 South Columbia, Tulsa, OK 74105.

# COWBOY/WESTERN MUSIC AND THE RADIO

*Guy Logsdon*

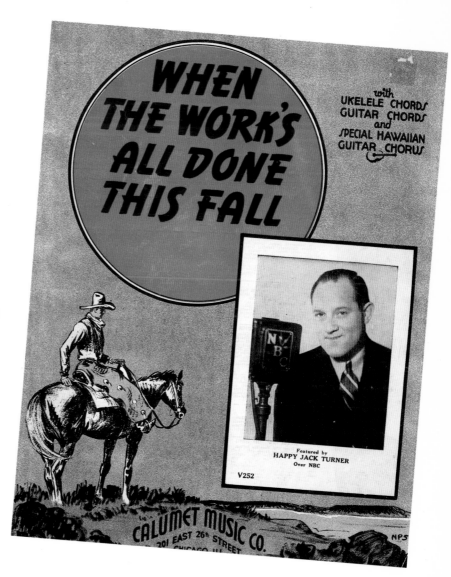

Commercial radio broadcasting as known today is approximately seventy-five years old, and little research has been done about its impact on traditional and country/western music. Archie Green, Bill Malone, Norm Cohen, Ed Kahn, and a few other scholars have included radio impact in their works, but no single in-depth study has been written. And limited information about memory retention among traditional and early-day country/western singers is known. The fact that these musicians relied on keen memory—often hearing a song once or twice over the radio and retaining the key lyric elements and melody—was primary to the transmission of songs.

Commercial radio broadcasting as we know it today started in 1920, and soon spread from the East Coast to the West. By late 1922, in Dallas, Texas, WFAA Radio featured Colonel William Hopkins, a fiddler from Kansas City, and a short time later broadcast the music of the Gibson Mandolin & Guitar Club. There was an indication that the music was or was not country/western in origin. However, in 1926, in Fresno, California, KMJ, which was a low wattage station, broadcast John Crockett, The Cowboy Singer.

Perhaps the first radio station to capitalize on rural music was KFKB, "Kansas First, Kansas Best," in Milford, Kansas. It was owned by the "goat gland" specialist, "Dr." John R. Brinkley, who used his station to sell his male sex rejuvenation transplant operation to husbands (often encouraged by wives) in the Plains and Mississippi Valley states. He broadcast a variety of programs including cowboy singers that appealed to small town and rural listeners, and in those days when there were not many broadcasters, low wattage stations were often heard over a thousand miles away.

In 1930, the Federal Radio Commission (now the Federal Communications Commission) forced Brinkley to sell the station. Farmers & Bankers Life Insurance Company purchased and moved it to Abilene, Kansas, with the call letters KFBI, reflecting the owner's name. In 1939, the station moved to Wichita, and after another change in ownership in 1964, the Wichita Great Empire Broadcasting, Inc. purchased it and formatted country/western music entirely with the call letters KFDI, using outstanding disc jockeys such as Johnny Western and Orin Friesen. Since then, Great Empire Broadcasting has expanded into Springfield, Missouri; Omaha, Nebraska; Shreveport, Louisiana; and Tulsa, Oklahoma—making it the most powerful country/western sound in the Midwest.

**Sheet music for "When the Work's All Done This Fall," Calumet Music Company, 1935. (Guy Logsdon and the Ranch House Library.)**

In 1926, the call letters were changed to KVOO, "The Voice of Oklahoma," and in 1928, oilman W. G. Skelly became sole owner of the station and moved all operations to Tulsa. The next year Gene Autry started singing over KVOO and appeared with Jimmie Wilson and His Catfish String Band. In 1934, Bob Wills and His Texas Playboys became KVOO members, later Johnnie Lee Wills and His Boys continued the western swing sounds. In the late 1930s, they broadcast the "Saddle Mountain Roundup" and featured many singers/musicians who later gained fame and recognition in the industry.

KVOO is now a station in the Great Empire Broadcasting chain and is probably the only radio station to feature two hours of western swing music each week. Disc jockey Billy Parker and the entertainment writer for the *Tulsa World*, John Wooley, host "Wooley Wednesday" each week, and the show is rebroadcast in the evening, beaming to all western states.

## "NATIONAL BARN DANCE," WLS RADIO, CHICAGO

The WLS "National Barn Dance" was first aired from the Hotel Sherman, April 29, 1924, as a pioneer in barn dance, ranch dance, stove/fireplace singing, and campfire music. Carrying its listeners back in time, it evoked fond memories of earlier, sometimes harder times. The program brought rural and urban listeners together in a musical romance with American heritage, and for nearly forty years, it introduced new cowboy/western and country-music to a widespread audience.

WLS Radio was created and owned by Sears, Roebuck and Company; the call letters stood for World's Largest Store. At that time, radio had to have live talent, so on Saturday nights they decided to book old-time music and cowboy songs. The show evolved from there, gaining enormous popularity. In 1928, Sears sold WLS to the *Prairie Farmer*, the nation's oldest farm newspaper. Sears took free air time as partial payment. The department store hired Gene Autry in 1930, and to promote his records, they put him on the "Barn Dance." He attracted new "western" talent such a George Goebel, who was billed as "The Little Cowboy"; Louise Massey and the Westerners; the Girls of the Golden West; Patsy Montana and the Prairie Ramblers; Eddie and Jimmy Dean; Pat Buttram; Rex Allen; Bob Atcher; and many more who went east instead of west.

Another station with a history of western sounds is KVOO Radio, Tulsa, Oklahoma. In 1924, R. H. Rollestone, an oil millionaire, wanted to promote his town, Bristow, Oklahoma, and established the station KFRU "Kind Friends Remember Us." The station officially broadcast in January 1925. They featured Jimmie Wilson and His Catfish String Band and Otto Gray and His Oklahoma Cowboy Band. Wilson and his group were businessmen from Salpulpa, Oklahoma, who played for fun and charity. They were the first to use sound effects on radio and the first to use radio waves for raising charity money. In 1928, they broadcast for twelve hours, raising money for sixty widows and children of coal miners killed near McAlester, Oklahoma. For information about Otto Gray, see the entry *Otto Gray.*

By the 1950s, as country/western music, radio stations, and listening habits changed, WLS was sold and turned into a rock station. The show moved to WGN and died in 1970.

## CRAZY WATER CRYSTALS

In the 1930s, the Crazy Water Crystals Company was the largest single promoter of country/western music (mostly hillbilly country), including on their local or regional radio shows such cowboys as Jules Verne Allen. The product they advertised and sold was crystals from evaporated water, the water coming from wells at Mineral Wells, Texas. The owners of Crazy Water Crystals Company capitalized on the worldwide search for health and aging cures in magical or mineral waters. While the crystals were originally used as a soothing mineral bath for tired feet, they became a laxative by the 1920s.

The first musical show Crazy Waters promoted was Dick Ware's harmonica playing in 1930. The entire Crazy Water history can be read in Gene Fowler's *Crazy Water: The Story of Mineral Wells and Other Texas Health Resorts* (Fort Worth: Texas Christian University Press, 1991).

## BORDER RADIO

This is the term used for radio stations just across the United States and Mexican border that broadcast with power as high as 1,000,000 watts—stations that could blast all others off the air. The man who gave birth to the idea of border stations was Dr. John R. Brinkley, who also professed to rejuvenate sexual power to impotent men by using goat glands. When the American Medical Association and the FCC ran him out of Kansas, he turned to Del Rio, Texas, and Villa Acuna, Mexico, for his base of operation. With Mexican support, station XEPN, "The Voice of the Western Hemisphere," was started in 1931. Other stations along the border from the east to the west coast of Mexico soon were broadcasting, and everything from sex rejuvenation to lifesize portraits of Jesus were sold. Cowboy, hillbilly, and religious music flooded the airwaves. For the complete story, read Gene Fowler and Bill Crawford's *Border Radio* (Austin: Texas Monthly Press 1987).

Starting in 1920 and lasting for four decades, radio was the primary method of disseminating cowboy/western music. Most stations in the West

GREETINGS FROM THE CARTER FAMILY
AND THE MAINERS
Carter Family, Top Row: A. P. Carter, Janette, Brother Bill, Sara, Maybelle. Children: Helen, Aneta and June. The Mainers, Standing: Ollie and Zeke. Seated: J. E. Mainer and Price.

PATSY MONTANA and LITTLE BEVERLY

COWBOY SLIM RINEHART

featured a western singer or western band, and Mexican border stations featured western as well as hillbilly musicians. Other singers heard the songs or purchased the songbooks sold over the stations and learned new cowboy/western songs. Indeed, cowboy/western music was perpetuated by the radio industry.

**A 1941 Border Radio advertisement. (Guy Logsdon and the Ranch House Library.)**

# Cowboy Music

*William Jacobson*

**C**owboy music is a true folk music created by cowboys for their own amusement. It may involve a borrowed melody or borrowed words, but it was written by cattle folk such as Curley Fletcher, Gail Gardner, and the late, great Anonymous; sung by cowboy singers Jules Verne Allen and Carl T. Sprague; and has been preserved by folklorists and cowboy folksingers, including Glenn Ohrlin, Guy Logsdon, and Buck Ramsey. When we speak of *western music* in this book, we are concerning ourselves with the tradition of polished material that was sung by the silver screen cowboys such as Gene Autry, Roy Rogers, and the Sons of the Pioneers, that was composed in Hollywood and Tin Pan Alley, and that is carried on today by Riders in the Sky, Sons of the San Joaquin, and others. *Western swing* is the appellation we give to the music originally based on the frontier fiddle music of Texas and Oklahoma, which also incorporates swing, jazz, and blues influences. As dance tunes, songs do not necessarily have accompanying vocals. The Wills brothers and Milton Brown were pioneers of the genre, and the tradition is carried on by, among others, Leon Rausch and Johnny Gimble, who played with Bob Wills, and The Pfeiffer Brothers and George Strait, who are influenced by earlier artists such as Milton Brown and Tommy Duncan.

What do the performers in these three categories have in common, besides wearing swell-looking western duds? Perhaps not much, originally, but now most cowboy and western singers and musicians incorporate elements of each in their performances, as well as other influences. Ray Reed once headed a swing outfit but is an authentic singer of traditional cowboy music. Ian Tyson writes beautiful songs that are sometimes equal parts cowboy, western, swing, and reggae. Chris LeDoux performs his original cowboy and western songs with a big rock sound. And Don Edwards sings in all three styles beautifully. Through their voices and instruments, these singers, musicians, and songwriters paint a portrait of the great American West. The finest cowboy and western music takes you way out West.

## What Is an Album?

Cowboy and western music was originally a strictly live phenomenon, followed by radio, 78s, 45s, extended playing 45s (EPs), long-playing records (LPs), reel-to-reel tapes, eight-track tapes, audiocassettes, compact discs (CDs), and digital audio tapes (DATs). Even more formats are at the door—optical discs, digital cassettes, and others!

From the late fifties to the late eighties, the long playing phonograph record was king, so sometimes the term "album" is incorrectly considered to be synonymous with "LP record." An album is a collection of songs. It might be a set of 78s, an LP, a cassette, or a CD. A single is one to three songs, while an EP (sometimes known as a mini-album) is usually four to eight songs. An anthology is a collection of tracks from singles, other albums, and sometimes previously unreleased material. A boxed set is the grandest of all, typically 12"x12" in size, holding several cassettes (LPs or CDs) and a deluxe booklet.

## Singing Western-Style Harmony Vocals

Vocal harmonies in the style of the classic Sons of the Pioneers are usually simple to arrange. The melody is sung by the lead vocalist, who may or may not necessarily be the most prominent singer. The tenor part is typically a major third above the lead. The baritone singer produces the fifth of the lead singer's note in the octave below the lead. If there is a bass singer, his part will be the same note as the lead, an octave lower. Together, the vocalists create a music chord.

In the key of C major (the white keys of a piano), C is the root, E is the third, and G is the fifth.

For instance, if the lead sings a C . . .
the tenor sings an E;
the baritone sings a G;
and the bass sings a low C.

Of course, these rules are not steadfast. According to the note sung in the song's scale, the mode (major or minor) of the scale, and the intended effect of that note (happy, sad, or tentative), the tenor singer might vocalize a minor third, the bass singer might sing a seventh, and the baritone might sing the sixth note, *ad infinitum*.

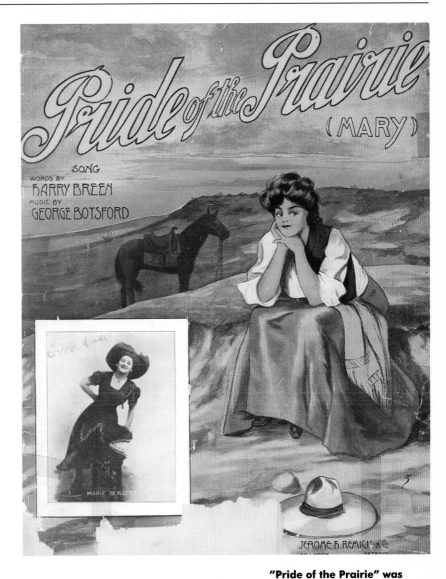

**"Pride of the Prairie" was published in 1907 by Jerome Remick and Company. (Guy Logsdon and the Ranch House Library.)**

**Sheet music for "I'd Like To Be In Texas For the Round Up In the Spring," Calumet Music Company, 1935. (Guy Logsdon and the Ranch House Library.)**

15

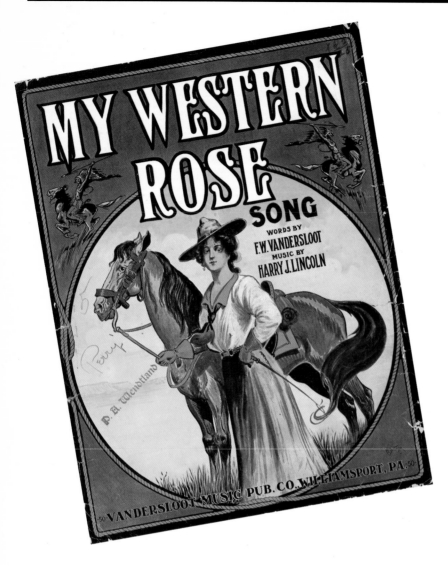

"My Western Rose" was published in 1910. (Guy Logsdon and the Ranch House Library.)

## THE WESTERN MUSIC ASSOCIATION

The Western Music Association was founded by Bill Wiley, who in 1988 threw a festival at the Union Hotel in Las Vegas. The organization, "dedicated to the preservation and enhancement of western music," is based out of Tucson, Arizona. Every year in late November, they hold a multi-day festival in Tucson, featuring many of the greats, past and present, of western music. Additions to a hall of fame are announced there, as well as the winners of a yodel and fiddle contest. The WMA also mails out the quarterly newsletter, *The Roundup*, to its members. For more information, contact the Western Music Association at 3900 E. Timrod, Tucson, Arizona 85711, (602) 323-3311.

## PATSY MONTANA
### (RUBY BLEVINS)
*Born in Hot Springs, Arkansas, October 30, 1914*

Patsy Montana is best known as the first female artist to have a million-selling record with her composition "I Want To Be A Cowboy's Sweetheart," which was recorded and released in 1935.

Montana was the only girl in a family of ten boys, which no doubt prepared her for her career in the male-dominated music industry. At age eighteen, she moved to California and sang on radio station KTMR. Although she played guitar and fiddle, it was her yodeling that caught the attention of

Patsy Montana (right) with Suzy Bogguss in 1991. Suzy a big hit with "I Want to be a Cowboy's Sweetheart." (Photo courtesy of Patsy Montana.)

Johnny Western. Courtesy of Richard Weize and Bear Family Records. (Courtesy song of the West.)

Patsy Montana. (Photo courtesy of Patsy Montana.)

# JOHNNY WESTERN

*Born in Two Harbors, Minnesota, October 28, 1934*

A striking singer with a resonant voice, Johnny Western began work in Hollywood as an actor and singer in the 1950s. He has worked with Johnny Cash, Gene Autry, Sons of the Pioneers, and Charley Pride. It only took Johnny Western twenty minutes to compose his signature tune "The Ballad of Palladin" for the television series *Have Gun, Will Travel.* Western also penned the themes for *Dodge City, Geronimo,* and *Bonanza.* Today, far from retired, he still tours and his baritone voice can be heard on radio station KFDI in Kansas. His albums include *Have Gun, Will Travel* (Columbia, 1962), with vocal backing by the Sons of the Pioneers, *Johnny Western Sings 20 Great Classics & Legends* (Americana), *Johnny Western* (JRC), and the massive four-CD collection *Heroes and Cowboys* (Bear Family, 1993).

Johnny Western with his 1993 Bear Family CD set. (Courtesy *Song of the West.*)

listeners and fellow entertainers. She proceeded to work with Stuart Hamblen on KMIC and with Lorraine McIntire and Ruby DeMondrum as The Montana Cowgirls.

Montana performed with the Prairie Ramblers (formerly the Kentucky Ramblers) on most of her recordings and on WLS's "National Barn Dance" in Chicago. She appeared in Gene Autry's horse opera *Colorado Sunset* (Republic, 1939). Among the labels she has been associated with are ARC (1934–52), Decca (1942–49), and RCA (1949–51). Her numerous awards include The Pioneer Award from the Academy of Country Music (1970) and induction into the National Cowgirl Hall of Fame, Hereford, Texas.

Patsy Montana has performed across the United States, in Austria, France, Germany, and the United Kingdom. She has dedicated her lengthy career to performing western music. She can be found at many cowboy and western festivals today, singing the songs that made her famous.

**GENE AUTRY** with *Smiley* **BURNETTE** *in* **'RANCHO GRANDE'**

*and*
JUNE STOREY
MARY LEE
DICK HOGAN
PALS OF THE GOLDEN WEST
BREWER KIDS
THE BOYS' CHOIR OF
SAINT JOSEPH'S SCHOOL
*Directed by Frank McDonald*

A *Republic*

Lobby card for Gene Autry movie *Rancho Grande,* released by Republic Pictures. (Guy Logsdon and the Ranch House Library.)

Gene Autry. (Guy Logsdon and the Ranch House Library.)

# Orvon Gordon "Gene" Autry

*Born in Tioga, Texas, September 27, 1907*

Gene Autry began his singing career as a five-year-old soprano in his grand-father's Baptist choir. At age twelve he paid eight dollars to Sears, Roebuck for his first guitar. Later he took a correspondence course in accounting and learned how to handle his finances. This financial ability combined with his musical talent made him not only the *premier* cowboy/western singer of his time, but also one of the nation's wealthiest men.

His father was a livestock trader who had western values but made little money. Gene's formative years were spent in both Texas and Oklahoma, and during that time, he worked as a farmhand, a ranchhand, a member of a medicine show, and a railroad apprentice. His railroad work led to a position as a relief telegrapher for the Frisco railroad and temporary work in Chelsea, Oklahoma. It was there Will Rogers heard him sing, and he encouraged Autry to record his songs.

For a time he sang over KVOO Radio in Tulsa, Oklahoma. From there he went on to the WLS "National Barn Dance" in Chicago as the "Oklahoma Yodeling Cowboy." His records sold in the Sears, Roebuck catalog, from which he purchased his first guitar, earning him a role in Ken Maynard's *In Old Santa Fe* (1934). The following year, he starred in the serial *Phantom Empire*, after which the concept of a singing-cowboy movie was developed for his talent. The first movie in this new genre was Autry's *Tumbling Tumbleweeds* (Republic Pictures, September, 1935).

During the following years, he starred in at least ninety movies, recorded hundreds of songs that made him one of the top-selling artists in recording history, served in the United States Army Air Force, starred on radio and television, purchased radio and television stations, became a major league baseball club owner, and created the Gene Autry Western Heritage Museum in Los Angeles.

Autry's life is chronicled in his 1978 autobiography *Back in the Saddle* (Doubleday & Co.) and can be heard on the award-winning radio documentary *The Gene Autry Story* (Champion Records, 1989, Gene Autry Western Heritage Museum).

**Trivia: In the late 1920s and early 1930s, Autry records were issued on different labels under these pseudonyms: John Hardy, Sam Hill, Tom Long, Overton Hatfield, Gene Johnson, Jimmie Smith, Bob Clayton, Johnny Dodds, and The Long Brothers (with Jimmy Long). In addition, Autry played guitar accompaniment for four George Gobel recordings on April 12, 1933.**

## Gene Autry's Cowboy Code

1. A cowboy never takes unfair advantage—even of an enemy.
2. A cowboy never betrays a trust.
3. A cowboy always tells the truth.
4. A cowboy is kind to small children, to old folks, and to animals.
5. A cowboy is free from racial and religious prejudice.
6. A cowboy is helpful, and when anyone is in trouble, he lends a hand.
7. A cowboy is a good worker.
8. A cowboy is clean about his person and in thought, word, and deed.
9. A cowboy respects womanhood, his parents, and the laws of his country.
10. A cowboy is a patriot.

**Gene Autry (left) and Smiley Burnette in a promotional still from *On Top of Old Smokey*, released March of 1953. (Guy Logsdon and the Ranch House Library.)**

## JOHN NICHOLAS "DICK" FORAN

*Born in Flemington, New Jersey, June 18, 1910*

Dick Foran was the second singer to assume the role of a cowboy in the new celluloid cowboy musical genre. Two months after the September 1935 release of Gene Autry's *Tumbling Tumbleweeds*, Warner Brothers released *Moonlight on the Prairie*, starring Dick Foran. It appears that someone in that organization had the same idea as Republic Pictures but was slow on the filming trigger.

Foran was the son of United States Senator Arthur F. Foran and was educated at Princeton University. He brought acting skills with him to Hollywood along with a strong, smooth singing style akin to that of Nelson Eddy, and he was the only singing cowboy to be featured by Warner Brothers. He starred in twelve films between 1935 and 1937 but never captured the imagination and following of the horse-opera audience.

In late 1941, he made a series of radio transcriptions with the Sons of the Pioneers, heard as the "Ten-Two-Four Ranch" for the Dr. Pepper Corporation; Foran was the range boss. Through the following years, he played different roles in over one hundred movies as well as being cast in a wide variety of television shows, from westerns to heavy drama.

He died on August 13, 1979.

## GEORGE HOUSTON

*Born in Hampton, New Jersey, in 1889*

George Houston, an easterner who attended Rutgers University, became a member of the American Opera Company before being cast as the star in a few United Artists musicals. In 1938, he starred in his first western, *Frontier Scout*, Grand National Pictures, and in 1940 he landed a role in the 1940 series *Lone Rider*, which included an occasional saddle serenade. He sang with his heavy operatic style and received no appreciative response from cows or audiences. In 1942, after eleven films, Houston rode out of the series. On November 12, 1944, he died of a heart attack.

**Dick Foran. (Guy Logsdon and the Ranch House Library.)**

## TEX FLETCHER
*Born in Harrison, New York, March 8, 1910*

Tex Fletcher's greatest success came through promoting himself. He starred in only one horse opera, *Six Gun Rhythm* (Arcadia/Grand National, 1939). Yet, he maintained a successful radio career as "The Lonely Cowboy," singing over WOR Radio, New York, for fifteen years, and he enjoyed moderate success in the early days of television. Through his own promotion, he made many personal appearances.

Promoters made claims that Fletcher was born on his father's ranch in South Dakota, but he was a New Yorker. He did cowboy in South Dakota and at one point in his career was part owner of a ranch near Lone Pine, California. Yet, most of his life was spent in New York.

Fletcher was a left-handed guitar player with a tenor voice. In 1936 and 1937, he recorded thirteen songs for Decca Records, and in late 1937 and 1938, he and his "Lonely Cowboys" recorded ten more songs, such as "Meet Me Tonight in the Cowshed." Also, two songbooks were published under his name, *Tex Fletcher's Songbook* (Joe Davis, Inc., 1937) and *Tex Fletcher's "The Lonely Cowboy" Songbook* (Stansny Music, Corp., 1940). He can also be heard singing "Yodeling Cowboy's Last Song" on the album *Cowboy Image* (MCA Records).

## SMITH BALLEW
*Born in Palestine, Texas, in 1911*

Smith Ballew was thought by many to be an extremely handsome man. He led one of the big bands during the late 1920s and the 1930s; in fact, Glenn Miller played trombone and worked as musical arranger for Ballew. However, Ballew was best known for his excellent singing ability, so it is believed that when Long Star Productions started the John Wayne *Singin' Sandy* series in late 1933, they turned to Smith Ballew. Supposedly, he sang the songs, and John Wayne mouthed the words while the cameras rolled, but some still claim this isn't true.

In 1936, Paramount Pictures hired Smith Ballew for a series of horse operas. The next year he moved to Twentieth Century-Fox, where he was cast as the lead in *Western Gold* and *Roll On, Cowboy*. He starred in enough features to make him one of the most popular saddle serenaders during the late 1930s. In the forties and fifties, he played supporting roles in many movies.

# COWBOY WORLD
## (THE NATIONAL COWBOY NEWS WEEKLY)
5c

**Tex Fletcher on the cover of *Cowboy World*, October 1945. (Guy Logsdon and the Ranch House Library.)**

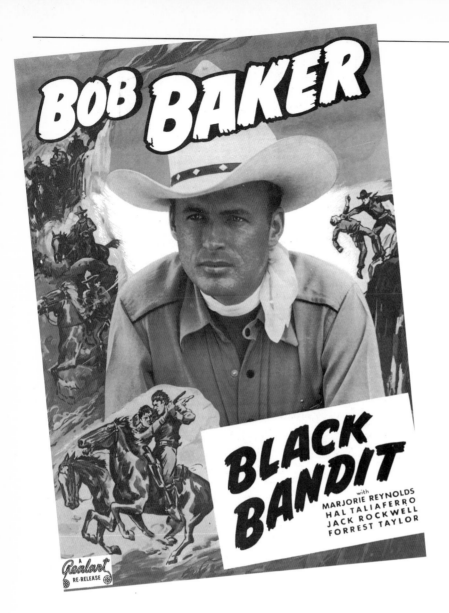

**Bob Baker's press book for the movie *Black Bandit*. (Guy Logsdon and the Ranch House Library.)**

## JAMES NEWILL
*Born in Pittsburgh, Pennsylvania, August 12, 1911*

James Newill grew up both in Pittsburgh and Gardena, California, and attended the University of Southern California, where he studied music.

In 1930, he became a member of the Los Angeles Opera Company. After traveling in a tent show, he became the featured singer on the "Burns and Allen" radio show and was the singer with a few big bands.

In 1937, he signed a contract with Grand National Pictures and played the title role in the series *Renfrew of the Royal Mounted.* He also rode through a few Monogram pictures and was featured in the *Texas Rangers* series, but as with other opera cowboys, the Saturday audiences did not respond to his singing. After dismounting from the singing cowboy saddle, he became a business man.

## ADDISON "JACK" RANDALL
*Born in San Fernando, California, May 12, 1906*

Jack Randall was enjoying a musical career on Broadway in the early 1930s, when his brother, western star Bob Livingston, enticed him to Hollywood. RKO gave him a contract and featured him in a few non-westerns.

In 1937, he signed with Monogram to be the star in cowboy musicals. He possessed a quality baritone voice, but as with most trained vocalists who tried to sing in the saddle, the production did not equal his vocal ability. It took only five movies to kill his singing-cowboy career. Still, he did remain in Hollywood, starring in nonmusicals as well as playing lesser roles. While filming some riding scenes on July 16, 1945, Randall died from a heart attack.

**TRIVIA: Former opera singers who tried to sing in the saddle: Fred Scott, James Newill, and George Houston.**

## BOB BAKER
*Born in Forest City, Iowa, November 8, 1914*

Bob Baker, originally named Stanley Leland "Tumble" Weed, may have been born in Iowa, but he grew up in Arizona and Colorado. He *actually* cowboyed and worked the rodeos before going to Chicago, where he became a member of the WLS "National Barn Dance."

In 1937, through his mother's efforts, he was given a contract by Universal Pictures and a new name, Bob Baker. Unfortunately, the new name did not bring new directing talent into musical B-westerns. A nice looking, pleasant, talented singer could not overcome the inability of bad directors, so after a few starring roles and a few lesser roles, Baker left Hollywood behind.

# John "Dusty" King

*Born in Cincinnati, Ohio, July 11, 1909*

John "Dusty" King, born Miller Mcleod Everson, attended Cincinnati University before working at a wide variety of occupations, eventually becoming an announcer and singer over Cincinnati radio stations WCKY and WKRC. He joined the Ben Berie Band as a singer in 1934.

In 1936, he moved to Hollywood, appearing in a few non-westerns. He was cast as a member of the Monogram Pictures' *Range Buster* trio with Ray "Crash" Corrigan and Max Terhune. After three years of limited singing and acting skills, he was thrown from the singing-cowboy saddle.

# Fred Leedom Scott

*Born in Fresno, California, February 14, 1902*

Fred Scott grew up on a California ranch and later studied acting and music in Los Angeles. He played roles in movies as early as 1929 before becoming a singer with the San Francisco Opera Company. Scott galloped off the opera stage in 1936 to become one of the early horse opera singing cowboys, starring in *Romance Rides the Range* (Spectrum Pictures). Over twenty western movies were made with Scott as the singing cowboy, but the production quality of his movies made it impossible for him to become a top-draw Saturday favorite.

Scott left the movie world in 1942 to work as a stage singer and later worked in the MGM sound department. He then entered the real estate business in Hollywood.

Songs from Scott's movie soundtracks were rounded up and edited by Ted Reinhart on the cassette *The Golden Corral* (Golden Corral, TERU 010).

Scott died on December 16, 1991.

# Lester Alvin "Smiley" ("Frog") Burnette

*Born in Summum, Illinois, March 18, 1911*

Known and billed as sidekick, Smiley Burnette was much more. His appearance in western movies attracted fans who would have ignored the featured actor. They went to the movies to see Burnette, for he had musical, comedic, and acting abilities, a combination few Hollywood stars could claim. He could play fifty-two musical instruments, some that he invented. In some movies, he played seven instruments at a

**Smiley Burnette in *The Blazing Trail*, 1949. Smiley is playing one of his homemade instruments with Hank Penny and Slim Duncan. (Guy Logsdon and the Ranch House Library.)**

time. He also wrote over 500 songs, including the classic "Riding Down the Canyon." Often these songs were used in movies.

Burnette showed interest in music at an early age and organized his own band in high school. After graduation, he eventually worked for WDZ Radio in Tuscola, Illinois. In 1933, Gene Autry, who had gained national popularity on the WLS "National Barn Dance," called Burnette to play accordion on the show. When Autry went to Hollywood in 1934, Burnette went with him. He appeared with Autry in Ken Maynard's *In Old Santa Fe*, then in Autry's *Phantom Empire* series, and at least eighty-one other Autry movies, playing the role of Frog Millhouse. He also appeared in seven of Roy Rogers's early films, helping Rogers's career, and in sixty-four Charles Starrett movies.

Along with roles in film, Burnette had roles in television and is best remembered as the engineer in *Petticoat Junction*.

Burnette recorded for his own label, Rancho Records, as well as for ARA and Bullet Records. At least two songbooks were published, including *Smiley Burnette: Cowboy and Western Songs* (M. M. Cole Publishing, 1937). Not only was he a musician, writer, actor, and singer, he was also a humanitarian who spent much of his money helping children in need. Smiley Burnette died of leukemia in Encino, California, February 16, 1967.

Tex Ritter in *Take Me Back to Oklahoma*. (Guy Logsdon and the Ranch House Library.)

# Maurice Woodward "Tex" Ritter

*Born near Murvaul, Texas, January 12, 1905*

Tex Ritter is best known for his performance of one of the most memorable Academy Award-winning songs, "High Noon." The song, his voice, and his interpretation made the movie a western classic. It was well-deserved recognition for Ritter, for in the saddle serenader world, no singer worked harder than he did.

Ritter attended the University of Texas, where he was influenced by cowboy-song collector John A. Lomax; cowboy-lore scholar and writer J. Frank Dobie; and voice teacher, composer, and publisher Oscar J. Fox. With voice training and a love for cowboy songs, Ritter eventually landed a job in 1930, singing and acting in the New York play *Green Grow the Lilacs*.

In 1933, Ritter joined "Cowboy Tom's Roundup," a children's radio cowboy show, and he recorded for the American Record Corporation. His rendition of "Rye Whiskey" became the standard version of that song.

Following Autry and Foran, Ritter became the third singing cowboy in the horse opera genre. His first starring role was in *Song of the Gringo* (Grand National, 1936), but that movie, as with most of Ritter's movies, was poorly financed and directed. He went on to star in many low-budget films, then shared top billing with others such as Bill Elliott and Johnny Mack Brown. He was in the top-ten B-western attractions but never made it to the number one position. Instead, his major role in cowboy music came from his recordings.

Ritter recorded a series of traditional cowboy songs for Decca Records in the 1930s and in the early 1940s became one of the first artists to sign with Capitol Records. The kinds of songs he recorded included cowboy, children's, country/western, and movie/television themes. His recording of "Blood on the Saddle" made it another western classic, but with the slow death of musical westerns, he moved to Nashville and became an early influence in the changing country music industry. However, he never left his roots in cowboy/western music. He died in Nashville on January 2, 1974, from a heart attack. Numerous Ritter recordings are still available, including *Tex Ritter: High Noon* (Bear Family, BCD 15634).

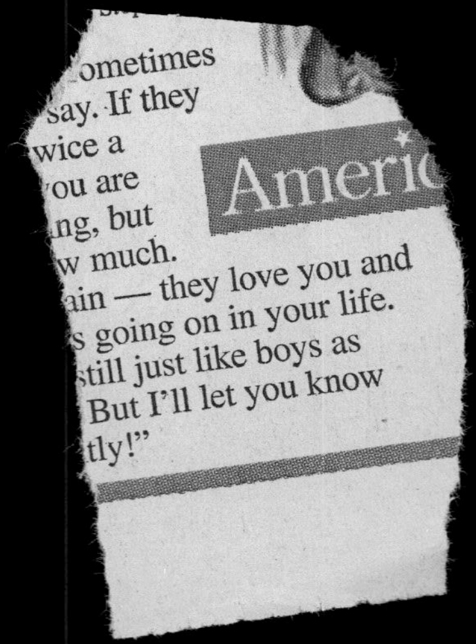

ometimes
say. If they
wice a
ou are
ng, but
w much.
ain — they love you and
s going on in your life.
still just like boys as
But I'll let you know
tly!"

Ameri

Lobby card for Tex Ritter movie *Rollin' Home to Texas*, released by Monogram. (Guy Logsdon and the Ranch House Library.)

Tex Ritter's sheet music for the movie *Rollin' Plains*, 1937. (Guy Logsdon and the Ranch House Library.)

## MONTE HALE
*Born in San Angelo, Texas, June 8, 1921*

**M**onte Hale possesses the Texan image: tall stature, broad smile, pleasing voice, and firm handshake. However, he does not consider himself to be a singing cowboy in the Autry-Rogers style, for he did not do as much singing in his movies as they did. Yet he did sing; in fact, he earned his ticket to Hollywood as a singer.

In 1944, Hale was working in Galveston, Texas, and by chance was hired to play guitar for a war-bond drive featuring a few Hollywood stars. This earned him a contract with Republic Studios and a few bit parts. His first starring role was the 1946 *Home on the Range* (Republic). It was the first B-western movie filmed in color by Republic. In his third movie, *Out California Way*, he was joined by Foy Willing and The Riders of the Purple Sage, who were in most of his movies. He starred in nineteen Republic westerns, and his singing-voice role was slowly reduced so that by 1949 there was no singing in his movies. His last starring role was in 1950.

Hale had limited success as a recording artist, recording for Beltone Records and MGM Records. It is unfortunate, because he had an excellent singing voice in his movies. After 1950, he appeared in other movies as well as on television and made personal appearances at rodeos; he still makes personal appearances at film festivals. He and his wife, Joanne Hale, who is executive director of the Gene Autry Western Heritage Museum, live in Southern California.

## EDWARD "EDDIE DEAN" GLOSUP
*Born in Posey, Texas, July 9, 1907*

**D**ean started his singing career in the late 1920s as a gospel singer in Texas, and in 1930 he and his older brother Jimmie started singing for radio station WIBW, Topeka, Kansas. After two years, Dean went to Chicago to act in radio serials and to sing for a short time for the WLS "National Barn Dance." He also appeared on station WNAX, Yankton, South Dakota. In late 1937, he left Chicago for Hollywood.

Dean knocked on doors for a year before he finally landed a small part in a Republic Pictures western, which opened the gate to other parts. While working at Republic, he appeared in over one hundred westerns with stars such as Gene

## LEON JERRY "JACK" GUTHRIE
*Born in Olive, Oklahoma, November 13, 1915*

**J**ack Guthrie is best known as the recording artist who introduced the classic western song "Oklahoma Hills." However, it was his cousin and good friend Woody Guthrie who composed it in 1937. Jack recorded it for Capitol Records, and it became a number-one hit in 1945. When Woody heard it on the jukebox, he called Capitol to get the copyright registered in both Jack's and Woody's names.

Jack worked rodeos until a back injury took him from the arena, and he played western dances up and down the West Coast. He was a popular singer, a successful recording artist, and a songwriter. When diagnosed with tuberculosis, he continued making personal appearances, wanting to ride the crest of popularity. Unfortunately, he died from the disease January 15, 1948, the same way his idol Jimmie Rodgers died. The most complete collection of his recordings is *Jack Guthrie: Oklahoma Hills* (Bear Family, BCD 15580).

**Jack Guthrie, 1944. (Guy Logsdon and the Ranch House Library.)**

Autry, Roy Rogers, Bob Steele, Bob Livingston, Red Barry, and others.

Dean sang in nine Hopalong Cassidy films against William Boyd's wishes, for Hoppy wanted no singers in his films. Also in 1944, he was featured in Ken Maynard's last movie, *The White Stallion* (Astor Pictures). His hard persistent work resulted in a starring role for PRC Pictures; in 1945, they produced *Song of Old Wyoming* in Cinecolor—Eddie Dean became the first singing cowboy to be featured in a color production and during the next three years starred in twenty cowboy musicals.

Dean's excellent voice received more praise than his acting, and he was in demand as a singing cowboy long after his movie career ended, recording for many labels such as Decca, Mercury, Capitol, and others. He wrote over a hundred songs and cowrote two classics, "One Has My Name, the Other Has My Heart" and "I Dreamed of Hillbilly Heaven." Dean and his wife, Dearest, live in Southern California and still make appearances at film festivals and events where saddle serenaders are loved and respected.

**Eddie Dean. (Guy Logsdon and the Ranch House Library.)**

EDDIE DEAN

**Monte Hale in the early 1950s. Guy Logsdon and the Ranch House Library.**

JIMMY **WAKELY** in *RANGE* **RENEGADES**
A MONOGRAM PICTURE

**Jimmy Wakely in Monogram Picture's *Range Renegades*. (Guy Logsdon and the Ranch House Library.)**

## JAMES "JIMMY" CLARENCE WAKELY

*Born near Mineola, Arkansas, February 16, 1914*

Jimmy Wakely was one of the few saddle serenaders in the 1940s and 1950s who enjoyed success in the movies, on the stage, over the radio, and on recordings. He was a hard-working, success-driven performer, who used music to raise himself out of the dust bowl-farming poverty.

When Wakely was three, his family moved to southeastern Oklahoma and later to western Oklahoma, where the dust bowl winds drove them back to Battiest and then to Rosedale in south central Oklahoma. Along the way, he learned to play the guitar and piano, skills that in 1937 landed him a radio job on KTOK, Oklahoma City, work in a

medicine show, and a singing role in the Bell Trio on WKY, Oklahoma City. He changed the trio to the Bell Boys by hiring Johnny Bond and Scotty Harrel. They were building a strong following when they went to Okemah where Gene Autry was scheduled for a parade appearance. Wakely approached Bill Slepka, who owned the Crystal Theater, and offered him a stage/radio broadcast show. He got an audition with Autry, who hired them and appeared on the show as a guest. The show was a sellout, and in September, 1940, Autry took them to Hollywood as members of his CBS "Melody Ranch Show."

After singing and/or working in movies with Gene Autry, Roy Rogers, Hopalong Cassidy, Tex Ritter, Johnny Mack Brown, Charles Starrett, and others, Wakely was signed by Monogram Pictures for his own western musical series. His first starring role was *Song of the Range* (Monogram, 1944). During the next five years, Wakely starred in twenty-eight westerns. By 1948, he was the fourth most popular cowboy singer/actor, and he started recording for Capitol Records.

His 1948 solo hit "One Has My Name, the Other Has My Heart" established him as a recording star, and when his movie career ended in 1949, he and Margaret Whiting recorded a few duets, including the number-one country and pop music hit, "Slippin' Around." That year Wakely was more popular than Frank Sinatra and Bing Crosby, and his popularity landed him in the CBS radio show "The Hollywood Barn Dance," which became the "Jimmy Wakely Show" and lasted through 1958.

Wakely established his own recording company, Shasta Records, and issued many of his radio shows and guest artists, making Shasta one of the most successful mail-order record companies in the 1970s. He also was a popular nightclub performer during the sixties and seventies. Songwriter, singing cowboy, recording star, radio star, record company executive, and nightclub performer, Jimmy Wakely died September 23, 1982. His biography was written by his daughter, Linda Lee Wakely, in *See Ya' Up There, Baby: The Jimmy Wakely Story.*

# KEN MAYNARD

*Born in Vevay, Indiana, (for publicity Mission, Texas, was listed as his birthplace), July 21, 1895*

Ken Maynard was the first singing cowboy in the movies, debuting in *The Wagon Master* (1930). Since he was featured for his acting and action-packed roles in the silent and early sound eras and since he predates the horse operas, Maynard has seldom been referred to as a singing cowboy, but he sang and played guitar, fiddle, and banjo in his sound movies. He also was the first to use a cowboy song for a movie title and theme, *The Strawberry Roan* (1933), and he introduced Gene Autry to the western audience with *In Old Santa Fe* (1934).

Maynard had one recording session with Columbia, March 22, 1930, and recorded eight songs learned from his cowboy, rodeo, circus, and stuntman life. Of the songs he recorded, only two were issued, and one, "The Lone Star Trail," became moderately popular. It can be heard on *Back In the Saddle* (New World). His tenor voice was accepted in the movies but was less pleasant on a phonodisc. After twenty years as a silent-screen and talking-movie cowboy, he finished his film career with *White Stallion* (1945).

Maynard died in California, March 23, 1973.

**Ken Maynard. (Guy Logsdon and the Ranch House Library.)**

## "Ken" Curtis Wayne Gates

*Born in Lamar, Colorado, July 12, 1916*

Best known for his role as Festus in *Gunsmoke*, Ken Curtis was also a pop singer and saddle serenader. The son of a rancher, sheriff, and fiddle player, Curtis developed a love for singing, eventually studying music in college. In 1939, he rode away from Colorado to Los Angeles and became an NBC staff performer.

In 1941, Tommy Dorsey hired him as the replacement for Frank Sinatra in the Dorsey orchestra and suggested he change his name to Ken Curtis. The following year he joined the United States Army and upon his return in 1945 was signed by Columbia Pictures to star in musical westerns, including *Rhythm Roundup* with Bob Wills. However, Gene Autry moved from Republic to Columbia in 1947, and Curtis was dropped. He soon joined the Sons of the Pioneers, filling in for Lloyd Perryman and later for Tim Spencer.

His first recording session with them was April 28, 1949, and can be heard on various recordings through 1957, even though he quit touring with them in 1953. He continued his acting career in movies such as *The Searchers* and in the television series *Paladin* soon followed by *Gunsmoke*, 1963 to 1975. Most of his Festus fans knew nothing about his singing ability, but he worked many rodeos as a singing Festus, creating new followers of his outstanding vocal skills. His last major movie role was in *Conagher*, filmed shortly before his death and released in 1991.

Ken Curtis died April 28, 1991.

## Johnny Bond

*Born in Enville, Oklahoma, June 1, 1915*

Johnny Bond was another small-town, self-taught musician who became a successful songwriter, cowboy singer, radio performer, recording artist, and music historian in Hollywood. Born in south central Oklahoma a few miles north of the Red River, he and his family left the farm to live in nearby Marietta where he attended school. During those school years, he developed a love for the music of Jimmie Rodgers, Bob Wills, and other pioneers in country/western music and taught himself how to play the guitar. When he graduated from high school in 1934, he moved to Oklahoma City and roped himself a nonpaying radio job as a member of a dance band, which led to his meeting Jimmy Wakely.

Bond and Wakely started singing together, and with the addition of Scotty Harrel, they became the Bell Boys, broadcasting over WKY, Oklahoma City, and KVOO, Tulsa, for the Bell Clothing Company. Bond composed his western classic "Cimarron" for the trio while living in the Oklahoma City YMCA. In 1940, they joined Gene Autry in Hollywood (see also Jimmy Wakely).

In Hollywood, Bond developed a reputation for humor and musical reliability in approximately thirty-eight movies, on the "Hollywood Barn Dance," and on Gene Autry's "Melody Ranch." His records were labeled, "Johnny Bond and his Red River Valley Boys" and featured Bond singing his songs, along with the songs of Merle Travis and other friends. Through the years, he recorded for Columbia, Republic, and Starday and wrote over five hundred songs. He cohosted the "Compton (California) Town Hall Party," a combined dance and stage show televised in the 1950s.

Later he and Tex Ritter were partners in a music publishing business, and he authored a Tex Ritter biography as well as his own story, *Reflections: The Autobiography of Johnny Bond* (Los Angeles: John Edwards Memorial Foundation, 1976).

Johnny Bond died of a heart attack, June 12, 1978.

**Rex Allen in a 1949 Republic Picture publicity still. (*Song of the West* collection.)**

**Johnny Bond, 1940. (Guy Logsdon and the Ranch House Library.)**

# REX ALLEN
*Born in Willcox, Arizona, December 31, 1921*

Rex Allen was the last to be signed as a Hollywood cowboy singer, and he is one of the few who actually grew up in a cowboy/ranch setting. He spent his youth on a ranch near Willcox and learned to play the guitar as backup for his father, who was a fiddler. As with many country/western singers, he gained experience singing in church.

As a teenager, Allen roped a radio-singing job on Phoenix's KOY; he also rodeoed for a short time. His rodeo competition took him to the East Coast where in 1943 a few disastrous rides left him broke in Trenton, New Jersey. He found a cowboy-singing job with Trenton radio station WTTM and later joined The Sleepy Hollow Gang in Allentown, Pennsylvania.

In 1945, Allen became a member of Chicago's WLS "National Barn Dance." His segment of the show was sponsored by Phillips Petroleum, and when he went to Hollywood in 1950, Phillips continued to sponsor him on CBS. His first starring-movie role was in *The Arizona Cowboy* (Republic Pictures, 1950), but by 1954 he was already dropped as a movie cowboy after making nineteen movies. He continued his radio show for a few more years and worked with Republic in the short-lived television series *Frontier Doctor*.

Allen has one of the best-known voices in America. After his acting career ended, he went to work for Walt Disney, narrating Disney's films with his smooth, deep voice. Because he has narrated over fifty films and hundreds of commercials, millions of people recognize the voice without knowing the man behind it.

Allen has recorded for Decca, Mercury, Republic, Coral, and other labels. His best-known album among the working cowboys is *Rex Allen Sings Boney-Kneed, Hairy-Legged Cowboy Songs* (JMI Records, 1972. Now available on the *Voice of the West*, Bear Family BCD 15284). For many years this collection of traditional songs was sold only in western clothing stores. He continues to make personal appearances at rodeos, film festivals, and benefits, because he still has one of the most distinctive voices in America.

## RAYMOND OTIS "RAY" WHITLEY
*Born in Atlanta, Georgia, December 5, 1901*

**R**ay Whitley was an electrician and steel worker living in New York City when the Great Depression hit, and there he was influenced by the success of Jimmie Rodgers. In 1931, he auditioned for WMCA Radio and was hired for a Crazy Water Crystals show as "Ray Whitley and his Range Ramblers." The following year he changed his band name to the Bar-Six Cowboys.

Whitley's recording career started in New York City with the Frank Luther Trio and in 1935 was featured on the "WHN Barn Dance" with Tex Ritter. By 1936, Whitley moved to Dallas and from there traveled to Hollywood with a contract to appear in a Hopalong Cassidy movie. This led to additional movie roles, often as a cowboy singer, and also led to his own filmed musical shorts.

Whitley collaborated with Gene Autry in writing "Back in the Saddle" (recorded by Autry in 1939) and in the early 1940s, while working on the "Saddle Mountain Roundup," KVOO Radio, Tulsa, he met Fred Rose. They cowrote a few songs such as "Hang My Head and Cry" and "Lonely River." In addition to writing songs, Whitley had his own western-swing band in the 1940s, managed Jimmy Wakely and the Sons of the Pioneers, and recorded western songs for Decca, Okeh, and other labels.

One of Whitley's greatest contributions to western music was in 1937, when he helped Gibson Guitar Company design and build the singing cowboy's favorite guitar, the Gibson SJ-200.

Ray Whitley died February 21, 1979.

Jimmy Long, the first partner of Gene Autry, in 1936.

## JAMES "JIMMY" LONG
*Born in Blevins, Arkansas, in 1889*

**J**immy Long was Gene Autry's first musical partner and the uncle of Autry's first wife, Ina Mae Spivey. Little is known about Long until 1920, when he started working for the St. Louis-San Francisco (Frisco) Railway Company. He was a dispatcher and trained new employees. It was in this capacity that he met Gene Autry.

Autry was an "extra operator" or relief telegrapher, when in January 1928, he was assigned to the station in Salpulpa, Oklahoma. Long was there to train him, and during the training session, they learned that they both enjoyed music and the singing of Jimmie Rodgers. They made music together and collaborated in songwriting, with Long actually doing most of the writing at that time. Their combined efforts in "That Silver-Haired Daddy of Mine" became Long and Autry's first million-sales record. Subsequently, their songs were published in *Gene Autry's Sensational Collection of Famous Original Cowboy Songs and Mountain Ballads* (Chicago: M. M. Cole Publishing, 1932), and *Gene Autry and Jimmy Long: Cowboy Songs, Mountain Ballads* (Chicago: M. M. Cole Publishing, 1935).

Long recorded a few songs with Autry and was a member of the WLS "National Barn Dance" from October 1932 to July 1934, when he returned to his Frisco job and his home in Springfield, Missouri.

Jimmy Long did not seek fame and fortune as an entertainer; instead, he lived quietly in Springfield until his death in 1953.

**Stuart Hamblen and His Gang. (Guy Logsdon and the Ranch House Library.)**

# CARL STUART HAMBLEN

*Born in Kellyville, Texas, October 20, 1908*

The fourth child of six in an itinerant Methodist preacher's family, Stuart Hamblen picked cotton in Texas to help support his family and in the process developed a love of music from listening to his black coworkers. He also worked on ranches in the Texas panhandle, learning a few songs from cowboys. By 1925, he decided to try his hand as a musician and wrangled a singing spot over Dallas and Fort Worth radio stations as Cowboy Joe.

Hamblen recorded a few songs for Victor in Camden, New Jersey, and decided that Hollywood was to be his cowboy-singer bedground. In 1930, he sang with the Beverly Hill Billies, but poor health abruptly ended that job. He went on to work for a few radio stations in the area and started writing his own songs, including the classic "Texas Plains." His natural ability as an entertainer earned him his own shows, "Covered Wagon Jubilee" and "Lucky Stars," making him the most popular country/western radio performer in Southern California.

While in California, Hamblen recorded a few tunes for Victor, and on August 3, 1934, he became the first cowboy singer to record for Decca Records, with "Poor Unlucky Cowboy" and "Texas Plains." Many years later he recorded for Columbia and RCA, but while he maintained steady sales, he never became a top recording star.

Hamblen was also a reciter of stories, poems, and a writer of sentimental songs such as "This Old House," which was written after he supposedly found a dead prospector in a mountain cabin. His classic religious song, "It Is No Secret," was one of the many in the sentimental genre, penned after he attended a Billy Graham revival. Through his songs, Hamblen was recognized as one of the early crossovers from western to pop music.

Hamblen also appeared in a few movies and even ran for the 1952 presidency on the Prohibition ticket. In the sixties, he retired from entertainment but returned to Los Angeles's KLAC radio in 1971, broadcasting his "Cowboy Church of the Air."

During his career he wrote over three hundred songs and recorded hundreds. He died March 8, 1989.

THE "BEVERLY HILL BILLIES"
COMPLIMENTS of

STANLEY FLOYD KILARR
**RARE-ARTS PRODUCTIONS**
1402 East Main Street
Klamath Falls, Oreg. 97601

**The Beverly Hill Billies. (Guy Logsdon and the Ranch House Library.)**

# BEVERLY HILL BILLIES (ALSO TARZANA HILLBILLIES AND PRODIGAL HILLBILLIES)

*Formed in late 1928 by Glen Rice*

When radio was the primary form of home entertainment, Glen Rice was the station manager of KMPC, Beverly Hills, California. After taking a two-week vacation, he returned, telling his radio audience that he had discovered a small community of hillbillies in the mountains, and they had agreed to perform for KMPC. The listener response was greater than expected; they believed the fabricated story, and the Beverly Hill Billies became major radio entertainment in Southern California. It was a band put together by Rice, and it became one of the most popular shows during their era.

The early members included Cyprian Paulette as Ezra Longnecker, Leo Mannis as Zeke Craddock and Zeke Manners, Ashley Dees as Jad Scroggins, Aleth Giles as Lemuel H. D. (Horse Doctor), Harry Blaeholder as Hank Skillet, Peggy Bauerfeld as Mirandy, Charlie Quirk as Charlie Slater, and Glen Rice as Tall Feller. The membership changed through the years with much fanfare and included Stuart Hamblen, Elton Britt, Lloyd Perryman, Shug Fisher, and others who went on to perform in different musical organizations.

The Beverly Hill Billies also appeared in the movies featuring Smith Ballew and made tours with him. After making hundreds of radio transcriptions, recording numerous songs, and appearing in movies, the Beverly Hill Billies disbanded in 1944. Later, they sued and received compensation for the use of their name in the television series, *The Beverly Hillbillies*. In 1958, they tried a comeback, but after six weeks they disbanded again.

# FRANK LUTHER (CROW)

*Born near Hutchinson, Kansas, August 5, 1900*

Frank Luther was a pioneer in introducing country/western music to urban audiences. By the mid-1920s he was a well-known concert and radio performer, who toured extensively in this country as well as abroad. Through the works of Vernon Dalhart and Carson J. Robison, urban audiences were listening to country and cowboy music, so Luther joined the trend. In 1928, he teamed with Robison, and they recorded as Bud and Joe Billings, the Highhatters, the Homespun Trio, Men About Town, and numerous other pseudonyms. Many of the names they used were also used by Vernon Dalhart.

During this time, Luther recorded for many labels, often cutting several records and singing for four radio broadcasts in a single day. His wife at that time was Zora Layman, and she along with Robison were members of the recording sessions. In 1934, he even teamed with Ray Whitley for a few recordings. He recorded so often, it is estimated that he cut as many as 530 records in one year and an estimated three thousand during his career.

By 1935, Luther was concentrating primarily on recording children's songs, including collections of cowboy songs for children. He later became the Decca Records executive responsible for producing children's songs. This was his final career move, and he stayed with Decca for many years.

He died November 16, 1980.

# GIRLS OF THE GOLDEN WEST

*Born Mildred Fern (Millie) Goad, April 11, 1913, and Dorothy Laverne (Dolly) Goad, December 11, 1915, in southern Illinois*

This yodeling, singing-sisters act was enormously popular in the thirties and forties. Since they were competing with other duet acts and numerous cowboy/western singers, it was necessary for publicity agents to sell them as true westerners. It was consistently reported that they were born in Muleshoe, Texas; in recent years, their birthplace changed to Mount Carmel, Illinois, which is possibly correct. However, they lived in Mount Vernon, Illinois, a few years before moving to East St. Louis, Illinois, where they sang on WIL as the Goad sisters before changing their names to Good. Dolly sang and yodeled the lead, and Millie harmonized both singing and yodeling. It is probable that they were the first successful act to yodel in harmony.

With a new name in 1930, the Girls of the Golden West went to Texas, where they broadcast live over the border station XER. They made their own western clothes and slowly added cowboy songs to programs. After a few months, they returned home and in 1931, joined the WLS "National Barn Dance" in Chicago, cutting their first recording for Victor Records on July 28, 1933, and eventually recording sixty-four sides. They toured with Gene Autry and other members of the Barn Dance, and developed a large following of fans. In 1937, they moved to Cincinnati's WLW and the Renfro Valley Barn Dance, Boone County Jamboree, and the Midwestern Hayride.

Dolly married the well-known Prairie Ramblers' fiddler and showman, Tex Atchison, and Millie married William McCluskey, who booked and managed the shows in Cincinnati. They eased out of performances by 1949.

**Millie and Dollie Good, The Girls of the Golden West, in 1937. (Guy Logsdon and the Ranch House Library.)**

RADIO — STAGE — PICTURES — OUTDOOR

**The Billboard**
The World's Foremost Amusement Weekly

15 Cents
20¢ in Canada

OTTO GRAY
Organizer and Manager of the Radio/Stage/Screen Attraction
"Otto Gray and His Oklahoma Cowboys"

**Otto Gray was the first western star to be on the cover of *Billboard*. (Guy Logsdon and the Ranch House Library.)**

# OTTO GRAY AND HIS OKLAHOMA COWBOY BAND

*Birth information not found*

This outstanding cowboy entertainment troupe has been relegated to two or three lines or completely ignored in most country/western history books, even though they were the most popular country/western stage act in the nation in the late twenties and early thirties. They were the first touring cowboy/western stage show featuring genuine cowboy songs, and they were probably the first touring group to use large custom-made Cadillacs for transportation.

The organization started as the Billy McGinty Cowboy Band in Ripley, Oklahoma. McGinty was a legendary old-time cowboy who served with Teddy Roosevelt's Rough Riders at the Battle of San Juan Hill. Around 1921, a group of men in the Ripley area formed a small musical group, gained immediate popularity, and asked McGinty to front the band. They were one of the first groups to perform on KFRU, Bristow, Oklahoma, and received letters from many states requesting appearances. They brought Otto Gray in from Stillwater as their manager and announcer. The original band members were McGinty, Gray, and John Bennett, fiddle; Dave Cutrell, mandolin; Nealy Huff, guitar; Alvin Mitchell, piano; and Ike Cargil, bass cello. But these men did not want to become professional touring musicians.

Otto Gray and his wife were trick ropers, and he had the additional skills of being a promoter and manager. He took the name and reorganized with his son and other entertainers, making Otto Gray and His Oklahoma Cowboy Band a hot radio and stage act. After developing a name over KFRU and KVOO, they spread their following at KFJF, Oklahoma City and from there went to Kansas City, playing stations along their way to New York City and the Roxy Theatre.

Their act included cowboy songs, popular songs, trick roping and whip popping, dog tricks, and trick musical instrument playing. They soon were working the show circuits such as Loew, RKO, and Fox, and over one hundred radio stations carried their shows. They recorded for Gennett, Pathe, Okeh, Vocalion, Columbia, and other record companies, and Otto Gray became the first country/western performer to have his portrait on the front cover of *Billboard*.

Their western clothes, combined with their popularity, had an influence on other performers departing from hillbilly attire and using the western image for costumes. This group played a major role in making cowboy/western music popular throughout the nation. In 1935, they slowed down their activities and disbanded.

# THE CALLAHAN BROTHERS (BILL AND JOE)
*Birth information not found*

Even though this duet came from North Carolina, they have a greater musical association with the West than with the East. In the early 1930s, the Callahan Brothers developed a duet yodeling style and sang a few cowboy songs that created a recording and radio audience.

By 1940, they were in Tulsa singing on the KVOO "Saddle Mountain Roundup," and from there moved to KRLD, Dallas. They were not cowboy singers, but they sang and recorded a few cowboy songs that are considered to be excellent renditions salted with duet yodeling. In 1945, they appeared in *Springtime in Texas* with Jimmy Wakely, and Bill Callahan became a West Coast bass-fiddle-session musician. They continued to work as a team into the early 1950s, when the new sounds of music moved them out of the growing industry.

# EMMETT MILLER
*Birth information not found*

Little is known about this singer and recording artist other than he was a major influence in country/western music. He worked in blackface minstrel shows, and his recordings in the 1920s included "Lovesick Blues," "I Ain't Got Nobody," and "Anytime." His band, the Georgia Crackers, included Eddie Lang, Tommy and Jimmy Dorsey, Jack Teagarden, and Gene Krupa—musicians any western-swing leader would have wanted.

Miller broke his voice into a mild yodel before Jimmie Rodgers ever recorded—Hank Williams's singing was almost identical to Miller's, and his blackface dialogue was copied by many entertainers. Emmett Miller may have influenced Jimmie Rodgers, but he definitely influenced, directly or indirectly, Bob Wills, Tommy Duncan, Hank Williams, Merle Haggard, and thousands of other country and western singers and musicians.

# THE PRAIRIE RAMBLERS
*Birth information not found*

Best known as the backup or session band for many Patsy Montana recordings in the mid-1930s, the original Prairie Ramblers were boyhood friends from Kentucky. Shelby "Tex" Atchison, Charles "Chick" Hurt, Floyd "Salty" Holmes, and Jack Taylor were first known as the Kentucky Ramblers over WOC, Davenport, Iowa. They were the Prairie Ramblers when they became members of the WLS "National Barn Dance." They left Chicago for station WOR, New York City, and later, a few months after returning to Chicago, they were the Sweet Violet Boys. Recordings were also issued under the name Blue Ridge Ramblers.

**The Prairie Ramblers and Patsy Montana in 1936. (Guy Logsdon and the Ranch House Library.)**

**Elton Britt in an RCA promotional photograph. (Guy Logsdon and the Ranch House Library.)**

Exclusive RCA VICTOR RECORDING ARTIST

# NOLAN "COWBOY SLIM" RINEHART

*Born near Gustine, Texas, March 12, 1911*

In the 1930s, Cowboy Slim Rinehart became a household name in rural American homes who tuned in to XEPN, Piedras Negras, Mexico, "Voice of the Western Hemisphere." He was a cowboy singer who sang a wide variety of songs and who had a natural ability to sell over the radio. According to his friend Dallas Turner, nobody could "move merchandise by mail" the way Rinehart did.

He became so popular that every border-radio station carried him, because his shows were usually recorded on sixteen-inch discs and broadcast as live shows. He used different names, and listeners would write saying that one singer was better than the other, though Rinehart was actually the only singer for each show.

Early in her career, Patsy Montana worked border-radio shows with Rinehart as did other personalities who gained fame as country musicians, but he loved working border radio and sold hundreds of thousands of songbooks to his radio fans. The king of border radio, Nolan was killed in an automobile accident on October 28, 1948, while on a tour in Michigan.

# JAMES "ELTON" BRITT BAKER

*Born near Marshall, Arkansas, June 27, 1917*

Elton Britt was recognized as one of the all-time great and influential yodelers, and he was awarded the first official gold disc received by a country/western musician in 1944 for his million-selling patriotic recording "There's a Star Spangled Banner Waving Somewhere." He gained his interest in music from his father who was a fiddler, and he learned to play on a Sears, Roebuck guitar.

When the founder of station KMPC, Los Angeles, was seeking authentic "hillbilly" talent, his scouts were directed to fourteen-year-old Britt. Within a week, he was on his way to California, where he became the youngest member of the Beverly Hill Billies.

In his twenty years of recording for RCA, he cut 672 single records and approximately sixty albums. Most cowboy/western yodelers gained some of their style, either directly or indirectly, from this high-pitched yodeler. Britt died June 23, 1972.

GREETINGS FROM THE CARTER FAMILY
AND THE MAINERS
Carter Family, Top Row: A. P. Carter, Janette, Brother
Bill, Sara, Maybelle.   Children: Helen, Aneta and June.
The Mainers, Standing: Ollie and Zeke.
Seated: J. E. Mainer and Price.

PATSY MONTANA and LITTLE BEVERLY

COWBOY SLIM RINEHART

**Cowboy Slim Rinehart in a 1941 Border Radio advertisement. (Guy Logsdon and the Ranch House Library.)**

STEREO

COLUMBIA ⦿ lp

MORE GUNFIGHTER BALLADS AND TRAIL SONGS MARTY ROBBINS

LITTLE JOE THE WRANGLER
SONG OF THE BANDIT
RIDE, COWBOY RIDE
STREETS OF LAREDO
MY LOVE
SAN ANGELO
PRAIRIE FIRE
FIVE BROTHERS
THIS PEACEFUL SOD
I'VE GOT NO USE FOR THE WOMEN
SHE WAS YOUNG AND SHE WAS PRETTY

## MARTY ROBBINS
### (MARTIN DAVID ROBINSON)
*Born in Glendale, Arizona, September 26, 1925*

Even though Robbins gained fame as a country singer, he also was a western singer. He grew up in Arizona hearing the songs and stories of his grandfather and father and was inspired to be a singing cowboy by Gene Autry movies. Following a three-year stint in the navy, he returned to entertaining in the Phoenix area and in 1952 recorded his first hit with Columbia Records.

He made a hit with rock-and-roll fans and was considered to be a crossover into that genre. However, his greatest hit was "El Paso," a western theme with Mexican guitar sounds. He rewrote the "Zebra Dun" into the "Cowboy in the Continental Suit," and recorded a series of *Gunfighter* albums that contained numerous traditional cowboy songs sung in the Robbins style. He died of a heart attack December 8, 1982, in Nashville, Tennessee.

**Album cover for Marty Robbins's *More Gunfighter Ballads and Trail Songs*. (Guy Logsdon and the Ranch House Library.)**

## CINDY WALKER
*Born in Mexia, Texas*

Cindy Walker is a premier writer of western songs and country songs, and for a few years, she also enjoyed a recording/performing career. While a young person, she performed as a dancer in Fort Worth and in 1942 traveled to Los Angeles with her parents, where she happened to see that Bob Wills and the Texas Playboys were in town. She called hotels until she reached O. W. Mayo, who gave her the opportunity to pitch a few songs to Wills, including "Dusty Skies."

Later Wills's hits written by Walker included "Bubbles in My Beer" and "Miss Molly." Her songs have been recorded by western, country, and pop performers, including Bing Crosby. She made Hollywood her home until 1954, when she returned to Mexia, Texas, where she still lives and writes.

## "RED RIVER" DAVE McENERY
*Born in San Antonio, Texas, December 15, 1914*

Best remembered for the years he spent singing over Mexican border radio stations, this cowboy singer started his radio career in 1935. His success took him to New York in 1938, and he broadcast over WOR, a Mutual Broadcasting System affiliate that sent his show nationwide. He used the byname The Texas Troubadour until the Swift Company sponsored his show for the 1939 World's Fair in New York; he became the Swift Cowboy.

In early 1940, Red River Dave recorded for Decca, using his radio band for the sessions, including Roy Horton, bass, and Vaughn Horton, steel guitar. For his live show audiences, he performed rope tricks as well as singing cowboy songs. As a songwriter, he became interested in current events and wrote "Amelia Earhart's Last Ride" along with songs about news events such as "The Ballad of Patty Hearst." During his career, Red River Dave recorded for Decca, MGM, and many small labels.

# THE RANCH BOYS

*Birth information not found*

This trio recorded for Decca Records between 1934 and 1937 and made personal appearances as late as 1940. The members were Joe "Curly" Bradley, whose real name was Raymond Courtney, guitar and vocal; Ken "Shorty" Carson, vocals; and Jack Ross, vocals. Most of their recordings were cowboy and popular western songs, but they did record a few pop songs. They made personal appearances from coast to coast and were featured on NBC.

Red River Dave in a Gretsch Guitar advertisement from *The Mountain Broadcaster and Prairie Recorder,* February/March 1947. (Courtesy of the Howard Wright Collection.)

The Ranch Boy songbook *Songs of the Plains,* 1939. (Guy Logsdon and the Ranch House Library.)

41

# LOUISE MASSEY AND THE WESTERNERS

*Birth information not found*

The Westerners, one of the most popular western bands in the thirties and forties, was a family band. Henry "Dad" Massey was the father of eight children, three of whom became professional musicians through his encouragement—Curt, Allen, and Louise. These three were born in Midland, Texas, before their father decided to buy the K Bar Ranch near Roswell, New Mexico. Curt, the oldest, was born May 3, 1910, and was taught to play the violin by his father. Dad Massey taught his other children to play a variety of instruments.

In the 1920s, the three children and their father were offered a contract to travel the Chatauqua circuit in the Midwest as the Massey Family Band, which they did for two years. While in Kansas City, they were given radio time and stayed there for a few years. Dad Massey went back to the ranch in New Mexico, and Larry Wellington took his place. Louise married a New Mexico musician, Milt Mabie, who became a member of the band.

After a few years in Kansas City, they joined the WLS "National Barn Dance" in 1928. From there they went to New York City and were featured on the radio show "Showboat." When that show moved to Hollywood, they stayed in New York with their own radio show, "The Log Cabin Dude Ranch." Their popularity took them across the nation on personal appearance tours before returning to Chicago, WLS, and the Plantation Party show.

During this time, they changed from the family name to "The Westerners," and with Louise becoming more and more popular as the vocalist, they changed their name to Louise Massey and the Westerners. They recorded for a variety of labels, and Louise is best remembered for cowriting "My Adobe Hacienda."

After disbanding, Curt continued his career in popular music and became the musical director and theme songwriter for the television shows *Beverly Hillbillies* and *Petticoat Junction*.

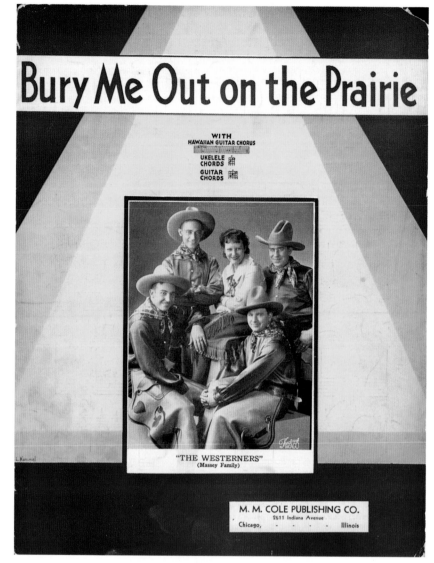

**Louise Massey and the Westerners sheet music for "Bury Me Out on the Prairie," 1932. (Guy Logsdon and the Ranch House Library.)**

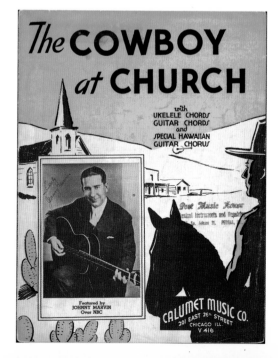

**Johnny Marvin sheet music for "The Cowboy at Church," 1935. (Guy Logsdon and the Ranch House Library.)**

# JOHNNY MARVIN

*Born in Butler, Oklahoma, in 1898*

It is told that Johnny Marvin ran away from home at the age of twelve to be an entertainer. He made his way to New York City where he became a popular Broadway performer and recording artist for Victor. He recorded his first song with Victor in October 1926, and in December, cut guitar duets with William Carola. He also recorded songs with his ukelele for accompaniment. He landed a radio show and became the "Lonesome Singer of the Air," using his brother Frankie Marvin on the show.

In 1929, Gene Autry made his way to New York, wanting to record his songs, and the Marvin brothers helped him while there. When Marvin's career waned in the thirties, Autry hired him as a songwriter and producer on the "Melody Ranch" show. Johnny Marvin died in 1945.

# FRANKIE MARVIN

*Born in Butler, Oklahoma, in 1905*

A younger brother of Johnny Marvin, Frankie followed Johnny to New York and became a member of his brother's show as a steel guitar player and comedian. In 1929, they recorded two sides for Victor as a brother duet. One cut was "She's Old and Bent, but She Just Keeps Hoofin' Along." He was the featured artist on a few recordings but fell far short of the number of songs his brother recorded.

In the early 1930s, Frankie joined Gene Autry in Chicago on WLS and later followed him to Hollywood where he worked with Autry until retirement in 1955. He played the steel guitar for Autry, giving a distinctive sound to Autry's personal appearances and recordings. Frankie Marvin was a major figure in the Autry organization.

**The Maddox Brothers and Rose. (Guy Logsdon and the Ranch House Library.)**

# THE MADDOX BROTHERS AND ROSE

*Birth information not found*

One of the most entertaining groups in the forties and fifties, the Maddox Brothers and Rose, were from Alabama, but the Great Depression drove them to California in the thirties. They turned their family musical talents into a way to survive and became a popular stage and recording act with comedy as a trademark.

Fred, Cal, Henry, and Don played a variety of instruments—guitar, fiddle, harmonica, bass fiddle, mandolin—while Rose sang most of the lead vocals. Their mother managed and booked them and had a reputation for being a tough taskmaster with her children. Their best-known recording was probably Rose singing Woody Guthrie's "Philadelphia Lawyer." When they disbanded, Rose continued to record as a single act and to entertain at music festivals throughout the nation.

## DALE EVANS
### (FRANCES OCTAVIA SMITH)
*Born in Uvalde, Texas, October 31, 1912*

Dale Evans, "The Queen of the West," has been the role model for many young cowgirls. Raised in Texas and then Arkansas, a bride at fourteen and a mother at fifteen, Frances began life early and enthusiastically.

Evans's initial professional goal was to be a pop vocalist with a big band. She landed work on radio programs and a role in Archie Mayo's film *Orchestra Wives* (1942). Her first appearances with Roy Rogers were in Republic's *The Cowboy and the Senorita* and *Yellow Rose of Texas* in 1944. The couple proved to be a popular draw at the box office, and Dale became Roy's partner in most of his succeeding movies. Her hopes of performing in swanky night spots was changed to the reality of singing while riding her horse Buttermilk on bumpy, dusty trails.

Dale married her leading man in 1947, and they have been partners ever since, professionally and personally. Dale's most famous western composition is "Happy Trails," the couple's theme song.

**Dale Evans. (Guy Logsdon and the Ranch House Library).**

## JENNY LOU CARSON
### (VIRGINIA LUCILLE OVERSTAKE)
*Born in Decatur, Illinois*

Jenny Lou and two of her sisters, Evelyn and Eva, joined the WLS "National Barn Dance" as the "Three Little Maids" and entertained radio and stage audiences until Eva broke up the group to marry Red Foley.

Jenny Lou actually started her career playing the tambourine and guitar on street corners as a Salvation Army lassie and continued as an entertainer who not only sang, but also performed gun, rope, and bull-whip tricks. She enjoyed a short career as a recording artist and gained her greatest success as a writer of western and country songs, such as "Jealous Heart," "You Two-Timed Me One Time Too Often," and "Let Me Go, Devil," recorded by Tex Ritter. She also wrote Eddie Arnold's hit "Don't Rob Another Man's Castle."

# THE FARR BROTHERS

*Thomas Hubert Farr—Born in Llano, Texas, December 6, 1903. Karl Marx Farr—Born in Rochelle, Texas, December 6, 1909*

Thomas and Hattie Farr had eight children and encouraged them all to play music. When Hugh was born, his father prophetically proclaimed that he finally had a fiddler for his family band. Soon enough, Hugh was able to participate in playing local dances and neighborhood parties with his family; such is the tradition in Texas. Younger brother Karl joined his sisters in playing the mandolin, then the banjo, and finally the guitar as he grew.

The family moved to Encino, California, in 1925. The brothers soon were appearing on radio. They went on to play with Len Nash and his Country Boys and Jimmy LeFevre's Texas Outlaws.

In 1933, Hugh was asked to join the Sons of the Pioneers. Hugh promoted the talents of Karl to the group, and Karl joined about a year afterwards. Along with backing them up instrumentally, the Farr brothers were able to record several of their tight fiddle and guitar tunes.

Hugh credits jazz and swing bands, rather than the usual country-style fiddlers, as a major influence on his playing. When brother Karl joined in, the Farr Brothers were an exceptional instrumental talent, blending jazz and Texas folk music into their own form of cowboy jazz. Improvisation was a specialty with the brothers, as they had played together all of their lives. Whether recording transcriptions or on stage, the brothers were never known to repeat anything twice.

Remaining a Pioneer for the rest of his life, Karl died of a heart attack while playing the guitar solo to "Up a Lazy River" during a performance in 1961. Hugh left the Pioneers in 1958 under less than amiable circumstances. He formed his own bands, even trying unsuccessfully to use the Sons of the Pioneers' name. He went on to front the Country Gentlemen and was still fiddling in the last years of his life.

**Jenny Lou Carson's songbook, published in 1944 by M. M. Cole Publishing Company.**

## ANDY PARKER AND THE PLAINSMEN

*Andy Parker was born in Mangum, Oklahoma, in 1913*

Featuring a vocal trio and swing instrumentalists, the Plainsmen were a popular western act in the Los Angeles area from 1944 to 1956. Andy Parker started his radio career in 1926, which continued for twelve years in the Midwest. Some time after moving to San Francisco in 1938, he landed the job of Singing Cowboy on NBC radio's "Death Valley Days." After a stint with "Dude Martin's Roundup" weekly on KGO, Parker moved to Los Angeles.

In 1944, Charlie Morgan, Hank Caldwell (also from the "Dude Martin Roundup"), and Andy formed the Plainsmen. Their songs were featured in a few Ken Curtis horse operas; the Plainsmen made their first screen appearance in Curtis's *Cowboy Blues*.

By 1946, Coast Records began releasing Plainsmen records. They began appearing on CBS radio's "Hollywood Barn Dance" and KNX, Los Angeles's "Sunrise Salute." Despite the band's success, Hank Caldwell left and was replaced by Paul "Clem" Smith, also from the "Dude Martin" show. At this point, they became known as Andy Parker and the Plainsmen. The group was signed to Capital Records, where they recorded over two hundred transcriptions, as well as many commercial recordings. Other achievements were numerous television and night club appearances, eight Eddie Dean movies, as well as the A-western *The Bashful Blonde from Bashful Bend* (Twentieth Century-Fox, 1949), directed by Preston Sturges and starring Betty Grable and Caesar Romero.

Singers and musicians who worked with the Plainsmen included Deuce Spriggens, George Bamby, Joaquin Murphey, Harry Simms, Noel Boggs, and Leroy Kruble. The Plainsmen went through many personnel changes, but when original member Charlie Morgan left the group in 1956, Parker chose to disband the outfit. Andy Parker's most famous composition remains the ethereal "Trail Dust."

**TRIVIA: Andy Parker, Charlie Morgan, and Marilyn Monroe sang the theme song in Otto Preminger's feature *River of No Return* (1954).**

# BOB NOLAN
## (ROBERT CLARENCE NOBLES)
*Born in New Brunswick, Canada, April 1, 1908*

The most poetic of all western songwriters, Bob Nolan has been a major influence on the rest of the field with his enigmatic compositions.

In the Settlement of Point Hatfield, 250 miles north of Saint Johns, New Brunswick, Canada, Bob Nolan was born to Harry and Florence Nobles. Young Bob spent his early years roaming the picturesque backwoods of remote Canada, but as he grew older, he needed an education, so he was sent off to Boston for schooling with his aunts.

After his father served in World War I, he moved to Tucson, Arizona, for health reasons, where he decided to change his last name to Nolan. At the age of fourteen, Bob took a long train ride to live with him. The freedom and movement of the train ride would become a recurring theme in the songs he would write.

The desert's beauty would also be a subject of his future work. Bob continued his schooling in Tucson and began his study of poetry. The works of Byron, Keats, Wordsworth, and Shelley were a strong inspiration. While still in high school in Tucson, he wrote a poem which was the basis of his classic western song "Cool Water."

In about 1927, he hoboed around the country, hopping trains and rambling for about a year. Nolan romanced free-spirited drifters in his first complete song, "Way Out There," as well as in many other early songs, such as "Tumbling Tumbleweeds" and "One More Ride." In 1928, he married Pearl Fields, and in 1929 a daughter, Roberta Nolan, was born. (He divorced Pearl in 1934, and married his second wife, Clara, in 1942.)

Nolan later rejoined his father, who had relocated in Southern California. There Nolan worked in a Chautauqua group and as a lifeguard on the sunny California beaches.

Bob Nolan answered Len Slye's *Los Angeles Herald* advertisement for the Rocky Mountaineers, who were looking for a yodeler. Soon, Bill Nichols joined them to form a vocal trio. After a time, Bob left the Mountaineers, as he felt negative about their future. A paying job caddying at the Bel Air Country Club seemed to him a better occupation.

Slye found him again in 1933 and convinced him to reenter the music business in Pioneer Trio with partner Tim Spencer.

The Pioneers, through the songwriting, arrangement, and sheer quality of their recordings and appearances, made substantial contributions to western music. Western music, as composed by Nolan, could be about the cowboy way of life, but just as likely concerned itself with frontiersmen or the rugged western landscape itself. Much of his work was poetry, for which he would compose a melody and harmony parts after he had written the words.

As a member of the Pioneers, Bob Nolan appeared in dozens of western films. The Sons of the Pioneers performed and recorded many wonderful Nolan songs throughout the thirties and forties, including "At the Rainbow's End," "The Boss is Hangin' Out a Rainbow," "Chant of the Wanderer," "A Cowboy Has to Sing," "Happy Rovin' Cowboy," "I Still Do," "Ridin' Home," "Roundup in the Sky," "Sky Ball Paint," "Song of the Bandit," "This Ain't the Same Old Range," "The Touch of God's Hand," "Tumbleweed Trail," "When Payday Rolls Around," and "Wind."

In 1949, three months after his good friend Tim Spencer left the group, Bob Nolan retired from appearances and live performances, although he occasionally recorded with the Pioneers through 1957. He continued to write poetry and songs. He had grown more and more dissatisfied with his association in the music business; he finally had enough and retired as a recluse in Studio City, California. This helped fuel the legend of Nolan as a loner and a detached figure.

Late in his life, he was coaxed by producer Snuff Garrett into recording a solo album, and in 1979 *Sound of a Pioneer* was released. The last track on it, "Wandering," summed up many of the themes from his work as a poet and lyricist and is one of the most beautiful country/western songs ever written.

On June 16, 1980, Bob Nolan passed away from a heart attack. He was survived by his widow, Clara "P-Nuts" Nolan, of Studio City, California, since deceased, and his daughter, Roberta Nolan Mileusnich, who resides in Las Vegas, Nevada.

At his request his ashes were spread across the Nevada desert.

**Roy Rogers, King of the Cowboys. (*Song of the West* collection.)**

# ROY ROGERS
## (LEONARD FRANKLIN SLYE)
*Born in Cincinnati, Ohio, November 5, 1911*

Roy Rogers, "King of the Cowboys," is one of the best-loved cowboy personalities in the history of cinema. Countless individuals cite him as a positive childhood influence. Though generally remembered as an actor portraying a singing cowboy, Rogers's career started with singing cowboy and western songs.

Young Len Slye was born into a closely knit, music-loving family who lived near Duck Run, Ohio. At seventeen, he took a job at a shoe factory alongside his father in Cincinnati. Dreaming of a better future in the midst of the Great Depression, Slye and his family joined his sister in California. He made his subsistence in Los Angeles driving trucks and later picking fruit in central California.

A move in 1930 brought Slye back to Los Angeles, seeking a living within the music industry. Joining the Rocky Mountaineers in 1931, he began appearing on radio shows. He placed an advertisement in a newspaper, hoping to find singers in order to improve the Mountaineers and found Bob Nolan at his door. Slye later added another vocalist, Slumber Nichols, and the group developed three-part harmonies.

In 1932, Bob left the Mountaineers, and Tim Spencer replaced him. After a brief time, Slye, Nichols, and Spencer quit the Rocky Mountaineers and joined up with the International Cowboys, appearing on radio. Later, with the O-Bar-O Cowboys and additional help from Cactus MacPeters fiddler Cyclone, they toured—better known as "barnstorming" in those days. A disastrous trip soon ensued, but young Slye met his second wife, Arlene, on his way through Roswell, New Mexico. Discouraged, the O-Bar-O's broke up; Slye and band went their separate ways.

Joining up with the Texas Outlaws, Len Slye, Bob Nolan, and Tim Spencer re-formed as the Pioneer Trio, also appearing on other radio shows as the Gold Star Rangers. Hugh Farr (fiddle) and brother Karl (guitar) soon joined up. Slye is credited with the formation of the Sons of the Pioneers. It was his energy and vision that developed the legendary group.

Slye was considered a master at cowboy yodeling, which is often overlooked today because of the other achievements of his career. His early yodeling on transcriptions and recordings is exceptionally original and innovative. Many of the solo yodels he worked out during this period are still used by contemporary singers, live and on recordings.

Len Slye had another talent—songwriting, often with Tim Spencer. Solid efforts such as "Song of the San Joaquin," "When the Moon Comes over Sun Valley," "In the Days of 'Forty Nine," "Down Along the Sleepy Rio Grande," and "Ridin' (in the Saddle)" can be found on transcriptions and recordings, which are revived by western groups now and then.

Fortunes soon flowed and the Pioneers appeared in Columbia movies starring Charles Starrett. Slye was also working bit parts on movies under the name Dick Weston. In 1937, Republic Studios needed a new singing cowboy because of the defection of Gene Autry. With the blessing of the Pioneers, Slye signed on with Republic Pictures' B-western movie factory and became Roy Rogers.

Adding to the musical career of Roy Rogers, the King of the Cowboys starred solo in a series of pictures, starting with *Under Western Stars* (also known as *The Washington Cowboy*, 1938). He continued doing musical shows between shooting pictures, which like his films and radio shows, always included western music. The Sons of the Pioneers would, on occasion, help provide musical backup and appearances for the pictures.

Slye recorded his first solo sessions in 1940 for Decca, a fully produced effort with love and popular songs. A cowboy in his fans' hearts, Rogers is most believable and poignant on western numbers, which he did record under the RCA label. Although appearing later in two non-Republic pictures, Roy spent life after the movies acting in over a hundred episodes of *The Roy Rogers Show* for television, which ran from 1951 to 1957.

Twentieth Century Records released Roy Rogers's last hit in 1974, "Hoppy, Gene, and Me," in which Roy bought into his own nostalgia. Rogers recorded a duet in 1990 with Randy Travis, "Heroes and Friends." RCA subsequently released the Roy Rogers *Tribute* album in 1991, in which Rogers paid respect to the Nashville country establishment.

**TRIVIA:**

**In 1962, The *Roy Rogers and Dale Evans Show* was a short-lived primetime musical variety show. This hour-long show lasted only three months and regulars included Pat Brady, Sons of the Pioneers, and Cliff Arquette as Charley Weaver.**

**Roy Rogers, Dale Evans, and Trigger. (*Song of the West* collection.)**

# Vernon "Tim" Spencer

*Born in Webb City, Missouri, July 13, 1908*

Often in the shadows of the enormous talent of Bob Nolan, Tim Spencer is also considered a major songwriter within the western field.

Born to a large family, Tim Spencer's father was a part-time musician who played the fiddle for social affairs. The church was Tim's own introduction to music in the form of singing. He was still young when his family settled in New Mexico. This had a great influence on his relationship with the West.

A few years later they moved to Picher, Oklahoma, where he continued his schooling. A disagreement with his father over the purchase of a banjo ukulele drove Spencer to move away from home, and he ended up working in Texas at the age of thirteen. After his father found him, they settled up and went home. When his schooling was complete, Tim worked in the mines. An accident ended that career, and he moved to music and playing in clubs. He had a fascination with western movies and the stars who inhabited that world, which led him eventually to take a Hollywood-bound train to find work in the business. His brother Glenn, already in Southern California, soon found Spencer at his doorstep. Working a day job at Safeway stores left him able to scout out the dances, clubs, and radio shows to find a musical opportunity. He joined the Rocky Mountaineers' Len Slye and Slumber Nichols as the tenor, even though his natural voice was lower, and he soon learned to yodel. During the infamous trip with the O-Bar-O Cowboys in Texas, he found his second wife, Velma Blanton of Lubbock, and married her in 1934. After returning to Safeway, he regrouped with Len Slye to recruit Bob Nolan from his golf caddie job to start up the Pioneer Trio.

Though Spencer hadn't written music until the Pioneers, he would be considered one of the best of the western composers. His first song was written for his bride Velma, "Will You Love Me When My Hair Has Turned To Silver." He later penned such classics as "Blue Prairie" (with Bob Nolan), "The Everlasting Hills of Oklahoma," "Timber Trail," and "He's Gone Up the Trail," among hundreds of other compositions.

Spencer left the group in 1936, citing a "difference of opinion," although he returned in 1937. Voice problems developed during the following years, perhaps because he had strained to sing in an unnatural range for his voice. Tapering off vocal duties as the years moved on, he retreated from performing and moved into the business end of the Pioneers in 1949. He found an appropriate replacement with Ken Curtis. His years after the Pioneers were spent forming and administering Manna Music, his gospel publishing company. Because of Spencer's illness, his son Hal took over the company in 1970. Tim Spencer died in Apple Valley, California, in 1974.

# Sons of the Pioneers

*Pat Brady—born Robert O'Brady in Toledo, Ohio, December 31, 1914. Ken Carson—born between Colgate and Centrahoma, Oklahoma, November 14, 1914 . Ken Curtis—born Curtis Wain Gates in Lamar, Colorado, July 2, 1916 . Tommy Doss—born in Weiser, Idaho, September 26, 1920. Karl Marx Farr—born in Rochelle, Texas, December 6, 1909. Thomas Hubert Farr—born in Llano, Texas, December 6, 1903. Shug Fisher—born George Clinton Fisher in Chickasha, Oklahoma, September 26, 1907. Bob Nolan—born Robert Nobles in New Brunswick, Canada, April 1, 1908. Lloyd Perryman—born in Ruth, Arkansas, January 29, 1917. Roy Rogers—born Leonard Franklin Slye in Cincinnati, Ohio, November 5, 1911. Tim Spencer—born Vernon Spencer in Webb City, Missouri, July 13, 1908. Dale Warren—born in Summerville, Kentucky, June 1, 1925*

When one generally thinks of classic western-harmony singing, the benchmark has always been the Sons of the Pioneers. There were western singers before them and after them, but the Pioneers had rare artistry and craftsmanship in their songwriting, arrangements, vocal, and instrumental performances. The original Pioneers were Len Slye, Bob Nolan, and Tim Spencer. Joining up with the Texas Outlaws, Slye, Nolan and Spencer formed the Pioneer Trio in 1934 and began appearing on radio shows. Slye was the lead voice and comic relief, Nolan was the group's baritone, and Spencer sang the tenor parts. The three singers developed a unique sound together. A hallmark of the early Pioneer sound was flawless three-part yodeling. The trio of young men rehearsed in a boarding house in Hollywood. They would sing until they literally began to drop. Spencer and Nolan began to write songs, which added to their repertoire. After a successful audition at KFWB, they were hired by Harry Hall, the station's staff announcer. Critical and popular acclaim soon won them their own program.

With Nolan playing stand-up bass and Slye on rhythm guitar, it was apparent that they needed musical help to accompany them. Hugh Farr's fiddle joined the trio in 1934, and his brother Karl, an outstanding lead guitarist, joined up in 1935. Hugh would later add his bass voice to the vocal blend.

Also in 1934, the Pioneers recorded a series of transcriptions for the Standard Company. Their name was changed that year when Harry Hall announced them on the radio as the "Sons of the Pioneers." He felt they were too young to be pioneers, and the name remained. That year found

them signed up with Decca Records, with whom they recorded from 1934–37 and 1941–43.

In 1935, film work started for them, including two horse operas with Charles Starrett and twenty-six other films through 1941. Over the years, the Pioneers would appear in movies starring Thelma Todd, Dick Foran, Bing Crosby, Gene Autry, Monte Hale, Eddie Albert, Ben Johnson, Spade Cooley, John Wayne, and Forrest Tucker.

By 1936, The Sons of the Pioneers quit their regular gig at KFWB in order to appear at the Texas Centennial in Dallas. Tim Spencer left when they returned to Los Angeles and was replaced by Lloyd Perryman. The following year Len Slye left the group to become Roy Rogers, "King of the Cowboys," for Republic Pictures. That year Rogers briefly came back to help them record some fine sides for American Record Company's Okeh and Vocalion Records.

In 1938, Tim Spencer rejoined the group. Some of the Sons of the Pioneers' finest performances were part of the Orthacoustic transcriptions—202 songs in total, recorded in 1940. Roy Rogers urged Republic Studios to have the group back him in his films. They sang and acted in these pictures, the first one being *Red River Valley* (1941) and the last, *Night Time in Nevada* (1948).

World War II saw Pat Brady and Lloyd Perryman leave for war duty. Taking Perryman's place was the adept tenor Ken Carson, and Brady was replaced by funnyman Shug Fisher. At the end of 1944, the Pioneers signed with RCA. Many fine singles resulted, including "Cool Water," "The Timber Trail," "Cowboy Camp Meetin'," "The Everlasting Hills of Oklahoma," "Chant of the Wanderer," and "Blue Prairie," among many others. Although Lloyd Perryman and Pat Brady returned in 1946, Carson continued to record with the Pioneers through 1947.

Tim Spencer retired in 1949, the result of vocal problems. Ken Curtis, later known as Festus on CBS television's *Gunsmoke*, replaced him. Pat

**Sons of the Pioneers when they were Farley's Gold Star Rangers. (Guy Logsdon and the Ranch House Library.)**

**Early Sons of the Pioneers—left to right—Hugh Farr, Karl Farr, Bob Nolan, Len Slye, and Tim Spencer. (*Song of the West* collection.)**

Brady left the Pioneer outfit to join as a sidekick in the Roy Rogers movies so Shug Fisher returned. Three months after his good friend Tim Spencer quit, Bob Nolan decided to throw in his hat. At this point there were none of the original Pioneer Trio left in the group, although instrumentalists Hugh and Karl Farr remained. Perryman assumed the unofficial leadership. He was the vocal arranger and on stage M.C. Tommy Doss, who had a dead ringer for Nolan's voice, joined in 1949.

In the following years, The Sons of the Pioneers produced some quality sides for Coral (1954) and returned to RCA. The record company tried moving the Sons into the pop market in an effort to boost sales. Their recordings in the 1950s became uneven as the western market went out of vogue. In 1952, they left RCA. Hugh Farr left the group in 1959. Two years later, Karl Farr collapsed and passed away during a Pioneer performance. Personnel changes continued and the Pioneers recorded a series of albums for RCA through 1969.

In 1972, Pioneers historian Ken Griffis and Pioneer patron Bill Wiley organized a great reunion gathering of Pioneers in Los Angeles. This would be the last time the remaining original Pioneers

would be on stage together. Tim Spencer died two years later; Hugh Farr and Bob Nolan were both gone in 1980, leaving Roy Rogers the only original Pioneer alive.

After the passing of Lloyd Perryman in 1977, Dale Warren assumed the leadership mantle. With appearances tapering off on the road, Warren developed the new concept of performing at a set place and having the audiences come to the act. Developing a nostalgia-laden show complete with multi-media presentation, the Sons of the Pioneers today are still playing "Tumbling Tumbleweeds" for their many fans.

Other members of the Pioneers have included Billy Armstrong, David Bradley, Rome Johnson, Gary LeMaster, Billy Liebert, Bob Mensor, Roy Lanham, Dale Morris, Luther Nallie, Tommy Nallie, Rusty Richards, Sonny Spencer, and Deuce Spriggins.

In 1979, the Smithsonian Institution designated the Sons of the Pioneers as a national treasure, and "Cool Water" and "Tumbling Tumbleweeds" were put into the National Archives. For more on the Sons of the Pioneers, see Ken Griffis's *Hear My Song: The Story of the Celebrated Sons of the Pioneers.*

## ART DAVIS

*Birth information not found*

Art Davis grew up primarily in Dallas, Texas, and started his swing-fiddle entertainment career at an early age. He was an original member of the band Roy Newman and his Boys as well as original member of the western string band, Bill Boyd and his Cowboy Ramblers, playing the fiddle in the first recording session of the Cowboy Ramblers on August 7, 1934, in the Texas Hotel, San Antonio.

In 1935, Davis left Dallas for Hollywood to work for Gene Autry, appearing in many Autry movies. He also worked in Bill Boyd's films in the early 1940s, and played major roles in two other movies. After World War II, Davis organized his own band, The Rhythm Riders. He appeared with them in the film *A Cowboy's Holiday*, released by Astor films.

Art continued his music career throughout his life, recording *Art's Music Memories* in 1981 with well-known Texas musicians Jim Boyd and Marvin Montgomery, just six short years before his death, January 12, 1987.

## HI BUSSE

(ENRIGHT A. BUSSE)

*Born in Warroad, Minnesota, August 6, 1914*

Hi Busse's start in show business occurred in 1933 when he tried out as a singer and accordion player for a new western group in Los Angeles. Jack Dalton, the band's leader, gave Busse the stage name "High Pockets" because of his great height. This new band, Riders of the Purple Sage, had a morning show five days a week on KFI. They played on the radio for six months, toured for six, then broke up. Busse started his own band, The Frontiersmen, in 1938. Over the years, they have backed many western artists on recording tours, including Roy Rogers, Eddie Dean, Rex Allen, Ken Curtis, and Tex Ritter. Hi Busse still performs with The Frontiersmen.

**Trivia: The Frontiersmen are the second oldest western group (the Sons of the Pioneers being the oldest) and the oldest western group that retains a founding member.**

**ART DAVIS** (STEREO)
**A COWBOY & HIS MUSIC**

I Wish I Had Died In My Cradle
Oklahoma Hills/Red Wings
Tamon Amore
San Antonio Rose
Nobody's Darling But Mine
In The Jailhouse Now
Waiting For A Train
I Wish I'd Stayed In The Wagon Yard
Bye Bye Blackbird
Lone Star Rag
Silver Haired Daddy Of Mine
Helping Someone Else

WHITE HAT RECORDS

**Art Davis on the cover of *A Cowboy and His Music,* released in 1975. (Guy Logsdon and the Ranch House Library.)**

**Hi Busse. (*Song of the West* collection.)**

**Bill Miller. (Photograph and hand tinting by Mary Rogers.)**

# BILL MILLER

*Born in Stockbridge-Munsee Indian Reservation, Wisconsin, January 23, 1955*

Bill Miller grew up on a Wisconsin Indian reservation in an environment of abuse, racism, alienation, and alcoholism, which are sometimes themes in his songs. He learned guitar as a youngster and found that folk music and the folk scene touched his sensibilities. As an adult he moved to Nashville and began going out on the road to play his music. Despite his less-than-ideal childhood, his music is often spiritual and inspiring. He sings in a gritty voice that is sometimes reminiscent of Bob Dylan's, and his soulful flutes and percussive guitar round out his unique sound. Miller is also a gifted storyteller, often using his guitar to embellish his tales to audiences.

After building up a following and putting out four independent albums—*Old Dreams and New Hopes; The Art of Survival; Loon, Mountain, and Moon;* and *Reservation Road*—Miller was signed to the Warner Western label in 1993, and the subsequent release of *The Red Road* confirmed his stature as an important contemporary recording artist.

# T. TEXAS TYLER

*Born near Mena, Arkansas, June 20, 1916*

T. Texas Tyler had the distinctive vocal style of growling during his songs. Though he started his career prior to World War II, it was after the war that he established himself in Hollywood where his popularity grew. He formed the T. Texas Dance Band and on January 11, 1950, NBC radio aired the first broadcast of his weekly show, "Range Roundup," from the Riverside Rancho. He was billed as the man with "a million friends."

His theme song, "Remember Me," was a hit song as was "Deck of Cards," "Dad Gave My Dog Away," and "Bumming Around." He recorded for Four Star Records, Capitol, Decca, King, and Starday, at times using session musicians, such as steel guitar player Speedy West, who were called "His Oklahoma Melody Boys." He appeared in western films, including *Horseman of the Sierras*. Later in life he experienced a major religious conversion and turned completely to spirituals and religious songs. He died in Springfield, Missouri, January 28, 1872.

**Sheet music for T. Texas Tyler's theme song "Remember Me." (Guy Logsdon and the Ranch House Library.)**

**Pioneertown O K Corral.**

**Pioneertown sound stage.**

**Pioneertown sign.**

**Pioneertown church.**

**Pioneertown Red Dog Saloon.**

**All photographs on this page taken by Vincent Lara.**

# OUT IN PIONEERTOWN

Tucked away in the low desert of California is a sleepy little dot of a hamlet called Pioneertown.

Like many Hollywood celebrities of the thirties and forties, the Sons of the Pioneers, along with Roy Rogers and other stars of the age, planned the development of a "city," west of what is now known as Joshua Tree National Monument. Conceived after World War II, these western entrepreneurs had high hopes that Pioneertown would be used by the studio industry in the productions of westerns, as well as having permanent residents. The song "Out in Pioneertown" was composed by the Sons of the Pioneers' Tim Spencer as a musical advertisement to help promote the town.

The song survives today, although Pioneertown is considered a failed venture. But, if you visit the area today, Pioneertown isn't entirely a ghost town. The remaining "Mane" Street and beautiful rock formation at the locale are instantly recognizable in some of the old television westerns such as *The Gene Autry Show.*

**The Beeman Brothers at Knotts Berry Farm, called Berry Place in 1940.**
(*Song of the West* collection.)

## THE BEEMAN BROTHERS AND SHIRLEY AND THE BEEMAN FAMILY

*Born Billy Beeman in Memphis, Texas, 1926. Bobby Beeman in Memphis, Texas, 1928. Don Beeman in Pampa, Texas, 1930. Shirley Beeman in Pampa, Texas, 1933*

The musical Beeman siblings first appeared on radio in Amarillo, Texas, for Cal Farley, broadcasting from the Tri-State Fairgrounds. The family also appeared daily in the Ford Motor Company Pavilion at the 1936 Texas Centennial in Dallas.

In 1937, the three boys went off to New York to work for show impresario Billy Rose in his production of "Frontier Fiesta" in Fort Worth. The Beeman Brothers went on to tour in 1938 with the WLS National Barn Dance Group, which included Eddy Peabody, Lulu Belle and Scotty Wiseman, Patsy Montana and the Prairie Ramblers, and The Hoosier Hotshots.

By 1939, five-year-old sister Shirley joined the band, playing slap bass fiddle, singing, and sharing M.C. chores with brother Bobby. They played with the "Kay Kayer Show" Sunday afternoons at Knott's Berry Farm in Orange County, California. The band came to an end in 1952, with one album produced for Broadcast Records in Chicago as well as numerous 78s—none have been rereleased. Currently a member of the Lobo Rangers, Billy is the only Beeman Brother now still performing.

## HERB JEFFRIES
*Born in Detroit, Michigan, in 1912*

Herb Jeffries was the first African American to play a singing cowboy in a full-length feature film. He began his career singing in Earl Hines's band in Chicago. Hoping to broaden his horizons, he moved to Los Angeles in 1937. After coming up with the idea of an all-black, singing-cowboy movie, he was cast in the lead role as Bob Blake. This role led to other motion pictures for him, including *Harlem on the Prairie* (1937), followed by *Bronze Buckaroo, Harlem Rides the Range, Two-Gun Man from Harlem,* and *Twenty Notches to Tombstone.*

After the movies, Jeffries toured with The Four Tones and his movie sidekick, Dusty. He was proud to be an African American and wore a white hat that was literally tied on because his hair was merely frizzy; he didn't want anyone mistaking him for a white man and once rejected an offer of portraying a Latin lover.

In 1939, he joined up with Duke Ellington. His biggest-selling record was "Flamingo" with Ellington (1941). He left Duke Ellington's organization because he knew that he never would see royalties as a dance-band singer. When Duke Ellington questioned Jeffries about leaving, he reminded Ellington that he had once done the same thing in his career. In the 1950s, Jeffries became quite popular as a performer on the French Riviera. Labels he has recorded for include Victor, Brunswick, Decca, RKO, Bluebird, Majestic, and MGM. In 1994, Warner Western released an album of Jeffries's recordings.

A true gentleman, Herb Jeffries's career has been an interesting bridge between white and black culture.

**TRIVIA:**
**At one time, Herb Jeffries was married to a Rose Bowl princess.**

# THE WAGONMASTERS

*Born in Memphis, Texas, 1926—Billy Beeman*
*Born in Memphis, Texas, 1928—Bobby Beeman*
*Born in Long Beach, California, 1936—Rachel*
    *(Cadwaller) Beeman*
*Born in Santa Maria, California, September 20,*
    *1939—David Bourne*
*Born in Kalamazoo, Michigan, July 3, 1935—*
    *Don Richardson*
*Born in Afton, Iowa, 1940—Vern Jackson*
*Born in Talihina, Oklahoma, 1937—Harvey Walker*
*Born in Long Beach, California, February 8,*
    *1932—Dick Goodman*
*Birth information not found—Jim Eisenberg*

From 1955 to 1968, The Wagonmasters were the company of musicians who appeared in the Wagon Camp at Knott's Berry Farm in Buena Park, California. Back in its early days, the theme park was a rustic family operation, and the ghost-town attraction was a perfect place to showcase cowboy and western music. A few albums were cut by this seminal collection of singers and musicians—most are in a variety of different cowboy/western groups these days. The tourists listened to more than 7,000 shows in the Wagon Camp and carried home Wagonmaster albums with them, which may have contributed greatly to the popularity of western music in many parts of the world. Today, the Wagon Camp is used for a cowboy stunt show. One such young boy who vividly remembers Knott's Berry Farm, the Wagon Camp, and the Wagonmasters grew up to carry on this music tradition—Ranger Doug Green of the Riders in the Sky.

TRIVIA:
**Dick Goodman and Don Richardson started The Reinsmen with Jerry Compton, Billy and Bobby Beeman, who later became members in The Lobo Rangers, and Harvey Walker, who has stayed on at Knott's Berry Farm in the entertainment division.**

**Masterson & Blackburn. (Photograph by Eric Weber.)**

# MASTERSON AND BLACKBURN

*Liz Masterson born in Denver, Colorado, December 8, 1946. Sean Blackburn born in Anoka, Minnesota, December 13, 1948*

Sean Blackburn performed on Garrison Keillor's radio broadcasts of "A Prairie Home Companion" from 1975–1981. He has been on several Flying Fish Records with Dave Hull before heading west and teaming up with Liz. She had toured for a season with Horse Sense as well as heading the Denver-based Cactus Crooners swing outfit.

As Masterson and Blackburn, Sean and Liz have performed at many poetry gatherings, concerts, and swing fests. Like Riders in the Sky, Ernie Sites and the Chambers, Masterson and Blackburn also perform children's shows.

Their collaborations include the self-released *Swingtime Cowgirl* (1988), *Tune Wranglin'* (1989), and *Kids at Heart* (1993).

## Roz Brown

*Born in Madison, Wisconsin, June 19, 1937*

One of the regulars at many of the poetry gatherings is Roz Brown. For over fourteen years autoharpist Roz Brown has been singing cowboy ballads, folk tunes, and sea shanties at Denver, Colorado's, oldest bar, The Buckhorn Exchange. His albums include *Colorado and the West* and *Just Kiddin' Around: "Music for Old Goats"* on his own Echo Lake label.

**Roz Brown on the cover of *Colorado and the West*. (*Song of the West* collection.)**

## Ed Montana

*Born in Detroit, Michigan, December 12, 1956*

Based in Amarillo, Texas, since 1990, Ed fronts the Coors Cowboy Band as an official representative of Coors Brewing Company. They play rodeos, state fairs, and other western events throughout the States. As a solo act, Ed has been touring European countries such as Germany, Austria, and Switzerland. His recordings include *Rodeo Man* (W-J Records, 1979) and, with the Coors Cowboy Band, *Cowboy Songs* (SROOC Records, 1983), *Step Into The Real Texas* (Six Pack, 1989) and *Six Thousand Miles* (Six Pack, 1991).

**Ed Montana. (Photograph by Lorrie Rittenberry.)**

# JOEY MISKULIN

*Born in Chicago, Illinois, January 6, 1949*

Joey Miskulin had a long and checkered career before he became known in cowboy and western music as "The Cowpolka King" with Riders in the Sky, Michael Martin Murphey's accordionist/keyboardist and the producer ramrod behind many of Warner Western's recordings.

Miskulin first appeared on an album in 1961 and has since toured, appeared, produced, and recorded various projects, including those of polka legend Frankie Yankovic and country veteran Johnny Cash, among others. He has produced over 200 albums.

Miskulin's first appearance on a cowboy/western album was on Gary McMahan's *Saddle 'Em Up and Go!* (Horse Apple records, 1988), where he was introduced to Riders in the Sky's Too Slim and Ranger Doug. Riders in the Sky featured Joey as their "orchestra" at live appearances from 1988 to 1990 and have utilized his talents on their "Riders Radio Theater" public radio broadcasts and television specials. This exposure brought him to the attention of Michael Martin Murphey, who featured Miskulin on his cowboy albums and in his live band. Miskulin has since produced Don Edwards, Waddie Mitchell, and Sons of the San Joaquin for the Warner Western label.

**Joey Miskulin. (*Song of the West* collection.)**

# MUZZIE BRAUN AND THE BOYS

*Born in Lewiston, Idaho, March 18, 1950—Muzzie Braun. Born in Sun Valley, Idaho: December 19, 1976—Cody Braun. March 5, 1978—Willy Braun. January 15, 1980—Gary Braun. August 15, 1981—Mickey Braun*

Muzzie Braun and his sons Cody, Willy, Gary, and Mickey are an entertaining family western music act. They won the 1990 Wrangler Award from the National Cowboy Hall of Fame for their album *Muzzie Braun and the Little Braun Brothers.*

They have appeared on the *Tonight Show* with Johnny Carson, and Cody Braun had a major role on the *Conagher* cable television movie that starred Sam Elliot and Ken Curtis of Sons of the Pioneers fame. Cody's role included playing his father's compositions on the fiddle. Their albums include *Muzzie Braun and the Little Braun Brothers; Ballads, Yodels and New Western Music; West-Tunes; and Big Town.*

**Muzzie Braun and the Braun Brothers, March 1993.
(*Song of the West* collection.)**

## THE LOBO RANGERS

*Born in Memphis, Texas, in 1926—Billy Beeman. Born in Santa Maria, California, September 20, 1939—David Bourne. Born in Boise, Idaho, June 26, 1944—Patty Bourne. Born in Denver, Colorado, October 29, 1951—Mike Fleming*

A rarity among most western harmony singing groups today, the Lobo Rangers specialize in performing strong original material and rarely heard western classics. Songwriter, fiddler, and mandolin player Billy Beeman had first teamed up with singer/guitarist David Bourne in the Wagonmasters in 1959. Dave and Patty Bourne have been singing together since 1963. Tenor vocalist and guitarist Mike Fleming, an accomplished songwriter, completes the band.

Their self-released albums include *The Last Cattle Drive* (1992) and *Stampede* (1993).

Cover for Robert Wagoner's *Heart of the Golden West,* painted by Robert Wagoner. (*Song of the West* collection.)

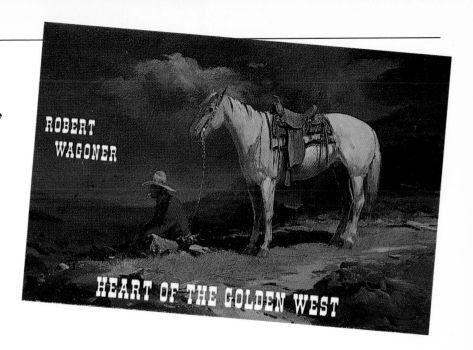

ROBERT
WAGONER

HEART OF THE GOLDEN WEST

# ROBERT WAGONER

*Born in Marion, Ohio, July 13, 1928*

Bob Wagoner came to California in 1939, where he taught himself the guitar at age fifteen. His first major gig was touring for two years with Tommy Duncan's All Stars. Other western acts he worked with in southern California included Ray Whitley, Billy Armstrong, Les Anderson, Merle Travis, Johnny Paul, and Hi Busse's Frontiersmen. Bob sang lead for the Reinsmen for a few years and in recent years had performed with Rusty Richards and the American Cowboys. Wagoner has written songs; his "High Country" was recorded by Tommy Duncan.

In 1960, Wagoner started an art career in paint and sculpture. He produces his own recordings in his own home studio in Bishop, California, by multi-tracking all of the parts himself. These albums, which demonstrate his rich singing voice and instrumental versatility include: *My Love Is the West* (1989), *Chant of the Wanderer* (1991), *I'll Take a Mule* (1992), and *Heart of the Golden West* (1993).

Trivia:

Robert Wagoner is best known for his Leanin' Tree card illustrations.

# Sourdough Slim
## (Richard Crowder)
*Born in Hollywood, California, November 26, 1950*

Sourdough Slim proclaims himself to be "Cowboy Music's Ambassador of Fun." Dressed in stylish pleated wool pants and a huge Stetson, Slim plays accordion, guitar, harmonica, and kazoo. His vocal style is reminiscent of the late Tex Ritter's, although it's much higher in pitch. The combined effect is a cowboy singer from either the twenties or thirties who has been strangely transported to the present day. Slim originally played in country-rock bands but moved on to bluegrass in the Eighth Avenue String Band, playing both guitar and mandolin. Just before the band broke up, he bought an accordion and learned to play it. He is an able songwriter, having written such tuneful songs as "Conestogas Ho!," "Ramblin' Cowboy," and "Cowpuncher Blues."

For live performances Slim sometimes performs solo and sometimes appears with his group, the Saddle Pals, which also includes Cactus Bob (Bob Cole) on fiddle, mandolin, and vocals, and Prairie Flower (Chris Stephenson) on acoustic bass, banjo, and vocals. Besides performing his songs, Slim and Saddle Pals perform material from the repertoire of Milton Brown, Carson Robison, Tex Ritter, and other cowboy/western music pioneers. The result in live performances is a giddy mix of music and comedy. Sourdough Slim's albums include *Just Risin'*, *Half Baked*, and *Western Skies* with the Saddle Pals.

**Sourdough Slim. (Photograph and tinting by Mary Rogers.)**

**Sons of the San Joaquin. (*Song of the West* collection.)**

# SONS OF THE SAN JOAQUIN

*Born in Marshfield, Missouri, February 1, 1931—Joe Hannah.*
*Born in Marshfield, Missouri, October 25, 1933—Jack Hannah.*
*Born in Pasadena, California, April 10, 1956—Lon Hannah*

Sons of the San Joaquin are a western vocal trio from central California's San Joaquin Valley. Consisting of brothers Jack and Joe and Joe's son, Lon, they truly are a family outfit. Joe Hannah sings lead, plays bass, and arranges the vocals; Jack Hannah sings the baritone and bass parts, plays rhythm guitar, and writes western originals; Lon Hannah sings tenor and plays lead guitar. Their talent is well respected by their peers and well loved by their audiences.

Jack and Joe grew up together singing the songs of the Sons of the Pioneers. Lon grew up hearing his father and uncle sing and convinced them to form a vocal trio when he was an adult. At this point, the Hannahs were making their living teaching and counseling at schools, occasionally riding horses and working cattle with their rancher friends. When Doc Denning, the Reinsmen's fiddler, heard them sing in 1988, he became a quick friend and provided them some musical direction to help their natural aptitude and potential.

In the summer of 1988, singer/songwriter Gary McMahan saw Lon sing at Bill Wiley's Western Music Festival in Las Vegas and convinced him that the Sons of the San Joaquin *had* to come out to Elko's Cowboy Poetry Gathering in the winter of 1989. At their first Elko musical session, their vocal power and purity was such an instant sensation that they were enlisted for a major evening performance spot. Later in 1989, Michael Martin Murphey flew the Hannahs out to Nashville to back him on his landmark *Cowboy Songs* album. With the ball rolling now, they released two independent albums, played around the West, and delighted cowboy and western music fans. The Sons of the San Joaquin were the first artists signed to Warner Western, along with Don Edwards and Waddie Mitchell.

In the early part of 1993, the United States Information Services employed the Joaquins as goodwill ambassadors on a tour of the Saudi Arabia Peninsula and Pakistan. As western good guys, they were an appropriate choice to represent America and cowboy culture.

With several television appearances under their belt, the Hannahs have helped reintroduce the classic style of harmony singing to national audiences. Like Riders in the Sky, Sons of the San Joaquin write and arrange new western songs, which undoubtedly will be present in their future albums. Their releases include *Bound for the Rio Grande* (1989), *Great American Cowboy* (1991), *A Cowboy Has to Sing* (1992), and *Songs of the Silver Screen* (1993).

**The Reinsmen, clockwise from top—Dick Goodman, Don Richardson, Jerry Compton, and "Doc" Denning. (*Song of the West* collection.)**

# THE REINSMEN

*Born in Long Beach, California, April 12, 1922—Max "Doc" Denning*
*Born in Long Beach, California, February 8, 1932—Dick Goodman .*
*Born in Kalamazoo, Michigan, July 3, 1935—Don Richardson.*
*Born in Santa Monica, California, November 5, 1935—Jerry Compton*

A western vocal harmony group, the Reinsmen are a veritable living museum of the original Sons of the Pioneers' sound. Dick Goodman, Don Richardson, and Jerry Compton founded the Reinsmen in 1962. This trio was the core of the Reinsmen's sound until 1993, when Don Richardson retired from the group. Other members of the group have included Bob Wagoner and Max "Doc" Denning, who possesses an appealing tenor voice reminiscent of Lloyd Perryman, as well as a fiddle style similar to Hugh Farr.

Besides keeping the live-performance tradition of the Sons of the Pioneers active, the Reinsmen have also written and recorded some western ballads of their own. Their albums include *Songs of the Trail* (Sierra, 1973), *Songs of the West* (Sierra, 1977), *Sentimental Trails* (Sierra, 1978), *Reinsmen: Alive In Death Valley* (Sierra, 1982), *This Ain't The Same Ol' Range* (Sierra, 1985), *Reinsmen: Collector's Edition* (a selective re-release of the first two albums), and *Don't Fence Me In* (Sierra, 1992). They also backed Don Edwards on his *Happy Cowboy* LP/cassette (Seven Shoux, 1977) and are on the soundtrack from the 1980 movie *Bronco Billy*. In addition, The Reinsmen made an outing on Rex Allen, Jr.'s, *The Singing Cowboy* album in 1982.

# RUSTY RICHARDS

*Born in Long Beach, California, November 15, 1933*

**B**orn in southern California, Rusty Richards grew up with the lure of the cowboy lifestyle tugging at him in his early years. He rodeoed and worked in both television and the movies as an actor and stuntman. In 1960, he recorded an album of folk songs for Jimmy Wakely's Shasta label. In 1963, the Sons of the Pioneers asked Richards to join them as their tenor. After twenty years with the Pioneers, he parted company with Dale Warren on strained terms. He went on to sing tenor on *Western Country* (Tower, 1976) and *Celebration, Volume One* (Silver Spur, 1982) with the Pioneers.

Richards also appeared on Cliffie Stone's *Country Hombres* (Tower, 1973) and recorded with Lloyd Perryman and Rex Allen, Sr., on "Can You Hear Those Pioneers," which appeared on Rex Allen, Jr.'s, *Ridin' High* album. While still a member of the Pioneers, he recorded *The American Cowboy* (Young Oak, 1984), a solo album of his own compositions. Occasionally he appears with The American Cowboys, a group consisting of Robert Wagoner, Dick Goodman, and Rusty. The amiable Richards has remained a horse trainer throughout the years and has practiced his cowboy skills lately at the Ben Johnson Pro-Celebrity Rodeos, winning many buckles. He has won many awards for his contributions to western music.

**Trivia: Rusty Richards was born in an emergency maternity ward set up in a eucalyptus grove next to Saint Mary's Hospital, which was damaged by the 1933 earthquake.**

**Rusty Richards. (*Song of the West* collection.)**

**Trudy Fair and Howdy, the world's most beautiful quarter horse. (*Song of the West* collection.)**

# TRUDY FAIR

*Born in Spokane, Washington, April 15, 1954*

**R**elative newcomer Trudy Fair specializes in the songs of the singing cowboys. Fair feels her most important achievement is "surviving twenty-two years as a musician." Her style is most evident on her album *I've Just Got to be a Cowboy* (Do It Your Own Darn Self, 1992).

# RIDERS IN THE SKY

*Born in Great Lakes, Illinois, March 20, 1946—Ranger Doug (Birthname—Douglas B. Green). Born in Grand Rapid, Michigan, June 3, 1948—Too Slim (Birthname—Fred LaBour). Born in Nashville, Tennessee, August 23, 1949—Woody Paul (Birthname—Paul Woodrow Chrisman)*

As singers, songwriters, musicians, and comedians, members of Riders in the Sky create western harmony in the true spirit of the original Pioneer Trio—they bring the sound, look, and sheer fun of the western-harmony groups of the thirties and forties radio shows and B-westerns to modern audiences.

Ranger Doug (baritone), Too Slim (lead), and Woody Paul (tenor) are a tight vocal trio with an inventive sense of arrangement. Too Slim's acoustic bass and Ranger Doug's rhythm guitar are a solid foundation for Woody Paul's imaginative jazz and country-influenced fiddle excursions.

Ranger Doug is a contemporary giant in the western songwriting field, rivaling the craftsmanship that Bob Nolan provided for the Pioneers in the thirties and forties. Too Slim is the soul of the group, with a whip-crack sense of humor. Woody Paul has been referred to as the *idiot savant* of the three, and his outstanding fiddle playing and songwriting has many admirers.

When the group began performing in 1977, few were playing western music on a national level. Bill Collins, and later Tommy Goldsmith, were vocalists/lead guitarists before Woody Paul signed up with the group. Their early shows were a bit racier than their current ones—the Triple X Ranch has become Harmony Ranch and questionable sheep jokes have made way for wholesome puns.

Riders in the Sky have been members of the Grand Ole Opry since 1982. In 1983, their series *Tumbleweed Theater* debuted on The Nashville Network. Each episode featured a classic B-western, a song or two performed live by the Riders, and a skit that involved characters such as Freddie L. A., Slocum, Drywall Paul, L. Philo "Larry" Mammoth, and the cantankerous, but lovable, Sidemeat.

Their Saturday morning children's show, *Riders in the Sky*, appeared on CBS television in 1991 and 1992, and National Public Radio has been broadcasting "Riders Radio Theater" since 1988. Riders in the Sky have appeared on albums with Roy Rogers, Kathy Mattea, Michael Martin Murphey, and Asleep at the Wheel. Among their many awards are the Wrangler Award from the National Cowboy Hall of Fame in 1990 for "The Line Rider" (Ranger Doug) and, in 1992 for "The First Cowboy Song" (Doug and Gary McMahan). Their albums *Cowboy Jubilee* and *Saddle Pals* have received Indie Awards from the National Association of Independent Record Distributors.

In their thousands of personal appearances, Ranger Doug, Too Slim, and Woody Paul, "American's Favorite Cowboys," have delighted young and old alike with "The Cowboy Way."

## A Selective Riders in the Sky Discography:

*Three on the Trail* (Rounder, 1979)

*Cowboy Jubilee* (Rounder, 1980)

*Prairie Serenade* (Rounder, 1981)

*Weeds & Water* (Rounder, 1982)

*Live* (Rounder, 1983)

*Saddle Pals* (Rounder, 1984)

*Western Songs* (Book of the Month Club, 1985)

*New Trails* (Rounder, 1986)

*The Cowboy Way* (MCA, 1987)

*Best of the West* (Rounder, 1987)

*Best of the West Rides Again* (Rounder, 1987)

*Riders Radio Theater* (MCA, 1988)

*Riders Go Commercial* (MCA, 1988)

*Horse Opera* (MCA, 1990)

*Harmony Ranch* (Columbia, 1991)

*Saturday Morning with Riders in the Sky* (MCA, 1992)

*Merry Christmas from Harmony Ranch* (Columbia, 1992)

*Cowboys In Love* (Columbia, 1994)

**Riders in the Sky. (Courtesy of David Skepner.)**

# MARION TRY "VERNON DALHART" SLAUGHTER

*Born in Jefferson, Texas, April 6, 1883*

In the summer of 1924, session guitarist Carson J. Robison was called into the New York City Victor studio to meet Vernon Dalhart and record with him "The Wreck of the Old '97." When asked for a flip side, Dalhart suggested "The Prisoner's Song." It sold 225,000 copies in four months and eventually sold over 25,000,000 copies. Thus, Dalhart and "The Prisoner's Song" have more to do with creating the commercially successful country/western music industry than any other performer, including Jimmie Rodgers and the Carter Family.

Born into a northeast Texas ranching family, Dalhart probably had a knowledge of cowboy songs before becoming a professional singer. During his teen years, he and his mother moved to Dallas, where he studied at the Dallas Conservatory of Music. Seeking a singing career, he moved to New York City and became a popular and light opera singer, combining two Texas towns for his stage name, Vernon Dalhart.

In 1915, Thomas A. Edison auditioned and

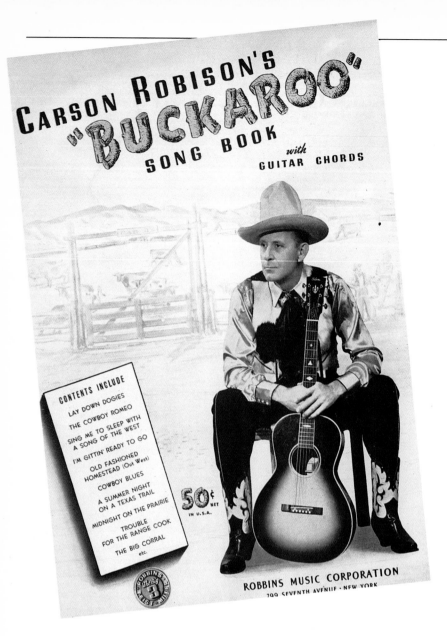

**Carson Robison on the cover of *Buckaroo* songbook, 1940. (Guy Logsdon and the Ranch House Library.)**

While most of his songs were "country," in April 1927, he was the first to record "Home on the Range," probably the best-known cowboy song, "I'd Like to Be in Texas When They Roundup in the Spring" (October 1926), and "Night Herding Song" (March 1927). He also recorded "When the Work's All Done This Fall," "Cowboy Lament," and other familiar cowboy songs.

Dalhart tried unsuccessfully to make a comeback in the late 1930s. He later became a hotel clerk in Bridgeport, Connecticut, where he died of a heart attack, September 14, 1948.

## CARSON J. ROBISON

*Born in Oswego, Kansas, August 4, 1890*

The son of a fiddler and dance caller, Carson J. Robison grew up surrounded by music. When he was old enough to make his own way, he tried railroading and oil field work, spending a few years in Tulsa, Oklahoma, where he worked for the Cosden Oil Company. Still, he always returned to music and, in 1920, moved to Kansas City, where he became a performer for radio station WDAF. He was one of the first cowboy singers to become a radio performer.

Robison left Kansas City for New York City in 1924, becoming a whistler for Victor; he could whistle two tones in harmony. For four years he also recorded with the first successful country/western recording artist, Vernon Dalhart, and by the late 1920s his NBC radio appearances as a cowboy singer along with his recording successes made him nationally famous.

As a songwriter, Robison used many themes, including cowboys and the West, and he wrote the ever-popular "Carry Me Back to the Lone Prairie." He wrote over three hundred songs, including the 1948 hit "Life Gets Tee-jus, Don't It?" Five songbooks (probably more) were issued using songs he recorded and/or wrote. Each was illustrated as a cowboy songbook.

Robison recorded for many companies, using at least nine pseudonyms. He also headed several bands: the Buckaroos, the Carson Robison Trio, the Pioneers, and the Pleasant Valley Boys. He was a creative songwriter who loved the romance of the West. He died on March 24, 1957.

signed Dalhart as an Edison recording artist. Until 1924, he recorded operatic and popular songs, then he convinced Victor to let him record a "hillbilly" song in an attempt to rejuvenate his lagging popularity. It was "The Wreck of the Old '97" that saved his career and Victor, for the company was also facing financial failure. He was the first country/western crossover and international star.

Through 1931, Dalhart recorded numerous songs that became the standards in country music repertoire, many written by Carson J. Robison about current events. He recorded approximately five thousand records for almost all existing record companies, using over an estimated 110 names. Over seventy-five million of his records were sold.

## Doie Hensley "Tex" Owens

*Born in Killeen, Texas, June 15, 1892*

The oldest of thirteen children, Doie Owens had one brother and eleven sisters in his sharecropper family. Even with no family music traditions, Doie became "Tex" and made his living as a cowboy singer/songwriter. His brother Charles cowrote a few songs with him, his sister Texas Ruby became a member of the Grand Ol' Opry along with her husband, Curly Fox, and his daughter Laura Lee (McBride) became Bob Wills's first female vocalist. However, before becoming a cowboy singer, Tex Owens worked at many occupations.

At age fifteen, Owens started working on ranches as a cook and cowhand and went on to work as a blackface minstrel in a medicine show. He also worked in the oil fields and as an auto mechanic, a bridge builder, and even as the town marshal in Bridgeport, Oklahoma. Along the way he was nicknamed "Tex." He married a Kansas woman and continued to work at different jobs, mostly in Kansas and Oklahoma (where his parents had moved), until he auditioned at radio station KMBC, Kansas City. He was hired and started his career as a professional musician.

For the next eleven years, Owens had his own show as the "Texas Ranger" and had a part in the show "Brush Creek Follies." While waiting for a KMBC broadcast in 1934, he wrote the ever-popular "Cattle Call," using a mixture of two old fiddle tunes for the melody. Different claims have been made about the song, but he is the songwriter who copyrighted it, and no one has proved he did not write it. It was included in a songbook published for KMBC, *Tex Owens, the Texas Ranger Collection of His Own Original Songs and Old Favorites* (1934).

After leaving Kansas City, Owens had shows on WLW, Cincinnati; KOMA, Oklahoma City; KHJ, Hollywood; and recorded for Decca and Victor.

In 1960, Owens and his wife moved back to Texas, where he died September 9, 1962.

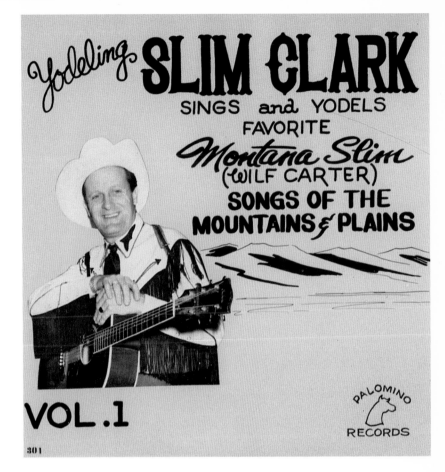

## Raymond Leroy "Yodeling Slim" Clark

*Born in Springfield, Massachusetts, December 11, 1917*

As a young man, Clark heard the radio shows of Wilf "Montana Slim" Carter and decided to ride the same yodeling/singing style. He started his radio appearances in his hometown in 1938 before moving to Keene, New Hampshire. However, it was in 1946 when he made his first recording for the Continental label.

In 1965, Clark started a series of long-playing recordings for Palomino Records. His songs were mostly cowboy and western songs marked by his brand of yodeling and were recorded in Maine. He is an example of how the popular idea of yodeling cowboys influenced the noncowboy world.

**Yodeling Slim Clark on the cover of *Yodeling Slim Clark Sings and Yodels Favorite Montana Slim Songs of the Mountains and Plains.* (Guy Logsdon and the Ranch House Library.)**

*The Singing Brakeman.*

## JAMES "JIMMIE" CHARLES RODGERS

*Born in Meridian, Mississippi, September 8, 1897*

Known as the "Father of Country Music," Rodgers was the son of a railroad man, and at an early age he also became a railroader. His musical background came from his coworkers—black railroad laborers—and when forced by health problems (tuberculosis) to seek work less demanding than railroading, he became a blackface minstrel.

In 1926, Rodgers and his wife moved to Asheville, North Carolina, where he started broadcasting over WWNC. The following year, Rodgers went to Bristol, Tennessee, where Ralph Peer and the Victor Talking Machine Company had set up recording equipment. On August 4, 1927, he recorded his first tune, "The Soldier's Sweetheart," which became a major hit and

established him as a recording star.

Rodger's influence on western music lies in a few cowboy songs that he wrote, such as "Cowhand's Last Ride" and "When the Cactus Is in Bloom," but more specifically in his yodeling style. While there is little evidence that cowboys used some falsetto vocal embellishment in their cattle calls, the use of yodeling in western music came from Jimmie Rodgers. In the late twenties and early thirties, numerous cowboy and western singers, such as Gene Autry and Tommy Duncan, were imitators of Rodgers.

Rodgers moved to Kerrville, Texas, where the climate was better for his tubercular condition, and while it may have given him a few extra months of life, he was not cured. He died May 26, 1933. For the complete story of Rodgers' life and influence, see Nolan Porterfield's *The Life and Times of America's Blue Yodeler Jimmie Rodgers* (Urbana: University of Illinois Press, 1979).

## GOEBEL LEON REEVES

*Born in Sherman, Texas, October 9, 1899*

**B**etter known as "The Texas Drifter," Reeves wrote and recorded a few cowboy songs in the 1930s. Hobo songs were his main interest, but the popularity of cowboy songs in that decade inspired him to devote some creative energy to writing and singing them, and, no doubt, his Texas heritage introduced him to cowboy culture.

One of six children born to a shoe-salesman father and a voice/piano-teacher mother, Reeves spent his childhood around music. His father was elected to the Texas legislature and moved the family to Austin when Reeves was a teenager. In Austin, he became enamored with hobo life and slowly moved into the life of an itinerant singer/songwriter with little to no contact with his family. He was a street singer in New Orleans and promoted himself into radio shows.

Reeves's first recording session was for Okeh in Dallas, June 1929, and the following year in New York City he recorded for Gennette. He had radio shows from Nova Scotia to Hollywood, appeared on the WLS "National Barn Dance" and the WSM "Grand Old Opry," was featured on the "Rudy Vallee Show," and had record releases on a variety of labels. Examples of his cowboy recordings are "Little Joe the Wrangler" and "The Cowboy's Dream" as well as his own songs, such as "The Cowboy's Lullaby" and "The Cowboy's Pal." He used many pseudonyms including the Yodeling Rustler.

He was a yodeler who had a distinctive style of vibrating his lips after yodeling, a style heard among Australian yodelers who were influenced by Reeves's recordings. He died January 26, 1959, in Bell Gardens, California. (The most complete study available is by Fred Hoeptner, "Goebel Reeves, The Texas Drifter," *Old Time Music* 18 [Autumn 1975]: 10-17).

## "TEXAS" JIM ROBERTSON

*Born near Batesville, Texas, February 27, 1909*

**R**obertson is another cowboy singer about whom little is known. He was a popular radio singer in the late 1930s and made appearances as late as the 1950s on the "George Hamilton IV" television show. Also, he recorded for Victor and MGM and possibly other labels, making personal appearances across the nation.

**Texas Jim Robertson on the cover of "Silver Dew on the Blue Grass Tonight." (Guy Logsdon and the Ranch House Library.)**

**Sheet music for Al Dexter's "Pistol Packin' Mama." (Guy Logsdon and the Ranch House Library.)**

# ALBERT "AL DEXTER" POINDEXTER

*Born in Jacksonville, Texas, May 4, 1902*

In 1942, Okeh Records released Al Dexter's "Pistol Packin' Mama"; it quickly became the top hit of the year, selling one million copies as well as two-hundred-thousand copies of sheet music. Bing Crosby recorded it for Decca, and he, too, sold one million records.

Dexter started working Texas clubs in the 1920s, using African-American musicians as well as Anglos and by the early 1930s was well established in east Texas honky-tonks. In fact, he owned different beer joints and was one of the first songwriters to use the term honky-tonk in the song "Honky-Tonk Blues." He recorded for Vocalion in 1936, changing to Columbia (Okeh) where he stayed for nineteen years. The record labels read Al Dexter and His Troopers or Texas Troopers, but the musicians used in the sessions were session musicians, not his band.

The success of "Pistol Packin' Mama" allowed Dexter to live comfortably near Lake Dallas and to operate his own clubs. Al Dexter died in January, 1984. For the story of how he wrote "Pistol Packin' Mama," see Nick Tosches, "Al Dexter," *Old Time Music* 22 (Autumn,1976) 4–8.

# PETER LaFARGE

*Born in Fountain, Colorado, about 1931*

LaFarge is best remembered for his songs "Ballad of Ira Hayes" and "As Long as the Grass Shall Grow." He was of Pima Indian heritage and was a poet, songwriter, dramatist, radio and recording artist, and rodeo rider. His father was Oliver LaFarge, the Pulitzer prizewinning author; his mother was Wanda Kane, and he grew up on his stepfather's ranch in Colorado. He learned cowboy songs from old cowhands and, as a teenager, came under the influence of folksinger Cisco Houston. He moved to New York City, where he recorded traditional songs and his own compositions about cowboys and Indians for Folkways Records; Bear Family Records reissued all of his recordings in 1993. Peter LaFarge died October 27, 1965.

# ARIZONA WRANGLERS
## (THE ORIGINAL ARIZONA WRANGLERS)
*Birth information not found*

This popular radio and stage group was billed as Sheriff Loyal Underwood's Arizona Wranglers during the late 1920s and early 1930s, broadcasting over KNX, Hollywood. In 1929, Curly Fletcher let them introduce his "Strawberry Roan" to their radio fans the way he wanted it sung, and in August 1929, they recorded it with "Nubbins" Frank Zeppino as the vocalist. They released it on October 20 as a special Christmas gift for $1.50 (information provided by Stanley Kilarr, Klamath Falls, Oregon).

The Wranglers were genuine working and/or rodeo cowboys who were not accomplished musicians, just good entertainers. The identities of the original group are not known, but in 1932, the Wranglers were J. E. "Nubbins" Patterson (not Zeppino), guitar; Charles "Irontail" Hunter, banjo; Cal "Sleepy" Short, harmonica; Laverne "Slicker" Costello, banjo; Joe "Hungry" Ivans, mandolin; Len "Dynamite" Dossey, fiddle; and "Sheriff" Loyal Underwood, emcee. Later, Clyde "Missouri" Copeland replaced "Hungry" as the mandolin player, and when they worked at the Phoenix, Arizona, Biltmore Hotel, Romaine Lowdermilk appeared with them.

In 1935, they appeared in the Universal movie *Stormy*, starring Noah Berry, Jr. It is not known when they disbanded.

**Very early Arizona Wrangler's Poster from the Howard Wright Collection.**

**Horse Sense in Papua, New Guinea. (*Song of the West* collection.)**

# HORSE SENSE

*Justin V. Bishop born in Denver, Colorado, November 28, 1950. John C. Nielson born in New London Boatyards, Connecticut, September 5, 1956*

A traditional band, Horse Sense has toured extensively, bringing old ballads, southwestern songs, and classic cowboy tunes to audiences around the world. Both are accomplished musicians. While singing their rustic arrangements, John plays guitar and banjo, and Justin plays mandolin and fiddle.

Justin and John's previous experience in presenting traditional music and folklore programs in schools, communities, and associations with folk arts residencies prepared them well to successfully bring Horse Sense to a wider audience than that of most cowboy and western musicians. The quality of their music and recordings comes from a gen-

uine love and respect for the music of the West.

Their unique *Hills of Mexico* is a *concerto grosso* for guitar, fiddle, banjo, mandolin, and orchestra. Written for the duo by Dr. Daniel Kingman, it was performed with the Camellia Symphony Orchestra and won an Indie (National Association of Independent Record Distributors and Manufacturers) award for Best Classical Release of 1986.

*Horse Sense for Kids and Other People* (1990) saw Horse Sense with Ted Smith on fiddle and dobro, as John Neilsen left the duo in 1989. The 1993 release *Ain't No Life After Rodeo* featured cowboy poet Paul Zarzyski and Richie Lawrence. Their albums include the following: *Songs of the Western Soil* (Kicking Mule, 1982), *Fences, Barbed Wire and Walls* (Kicking Mule, 1985), *The Hills of Mexico* (Kicking Mule, 1986), *The Colorado Trail* (Kicking Mule, 1989), *Horse Sense for Kids and Other People* (Music for Little People, 1990), and *Ain't No Life After Rodeo* (1993).

# Pondering the Relationship between the Cowboy Image and Music or Why Are All Those Cowboys from Nashville Singing Country Songs?

Mary Rogers and William Jacobson

**"Country and western is neither of either"**
Katie Lee

Sheet music for "San Antonio Song," Jerome H. Remick and Company (1907). (Guy Logsdon and the Ranch House Library.)

There are working cowboys today battling horses and cattle in the West, making a living that provides them great pride. It isn't the pay; it isn't the working conditions. It has more to do with the open spaces and the history of their cowboy heritage. They are more likely to take inspiration from the lore of the old vaqueros than from modern rodeo contestants.

The music they listen to is most likely traditional, also, by cowboy singers who, like them, honor the independent legacy of the cowboy and the West. Many modern saddle serenaders make an independent livelihood producing their own albums and marketing it themselves.

But everywhere you read or you look, the media is calling all of the young bucks from Nashville "cowboys." Early country performers appropriated the western theme and cowboy image to dissipate the notion that they were mere "hillbilly" performers (as they were known before the appellation "country"). From the 1920s through the 1940s, tall-in-the-saddle western heroes were the rage at picture shows across the land, and almost everyone loved the heroic image that filled the screen. From 1925 to 1935, Otto Gray and the Oklahoma Cowboys toured nationally with a western stage show that included whip and rope tricks and, of course, cowboy and western music. Early photos of Jimmie Rodgers in a sombrero and chaps clearly show the cowboy mystique at work.

This fashion continued through the era of Hank Williams and his Drifting Cowboys to the herds of cowboy-styled country stars that have paraded in boots and hats across the Grand Ole Opry stage throughout the decades. This is purely fashion, for we all know that cowboy and western music rarely is part of the Nashville sound, Riders in the Sky excepted.

Boot, shirt, and jeans manufacturers pay high-profile country stars large amounts of money to endorse their products. Audiences are confused with the sounds coming from this modern "cowboy" image on their television sets. Cowboy and western singers are usually found entertaining in more traditional clothing. Most Nashville stars look more like the rodeo athletes of today, wearing shirts sewn of a garish print and a pair of flat-heeled boots. Hat styles on cowboy singers tend to favor classic individual creases and brims. Country stars' hats lean toward more conservative modern stylings. More than one aging country star has found that a cowboy hat is a dandy way to hide a balding head.

# COWBOY YODELING

by Gary McMahan

Ah, the cowboy yodel—flowing, laughing, bubbling, then perhaps strangely still and dark yet crystal clear, always as clean as a mountain stream. Silvery and languorous, wafting down the canyon, it can win the heart of a maiden or, if you want to bear down on it, drill a hole through a Douglas fir. It can be used in numerous other ways: you can get served rather quickly in crowded restaurants ("Feed that yayhoo and get him outta here; he's not a well man."), call coyotes (everyone laughs at this, but they do actually answer back and come closer . . . I've done it many times!), and don't forget the echoes when you're out riding. I know of a place where you can, in round-robin fashion, yodel in harmony to yourself. But mainly what a yodel does, be it fast or slow, is to immediately instill a feeling in the heart of the listener (which does the same thing, by the way, to the singer). It can bring immediate joy as in the case of a happy yodel; a comforting dreamy warmth as in, let's say, Tex Owens's "The Cattle Call"; or blow a lonesome, chilly wind through your heart as in a well-done blue yodel.

I suggest the yodel is a form of spiritual communication that works in quite the same fashion as a poem. The rhyme and meter speak to you much more deeply than if someone just told you the plot and all the implications. A better example yet would be a song whose basic ingredients are lyrics and music. Neither alone has the power to reach the inner currents and winds of the soul as they do together. Take that old western song, Bob Nolan's "Way Out There." Try first speaking the lyrics. Then add music and sing the lyrics but without the yodel. Finally, add the yodel. Do you savvy? The power gained by adding each ingredient increases dramatically until you finally reach what I call "$Y^2$" (Yodel Squared). This is the state in which you multiply the spiritual communication of song many times over by combining lyrics and music and yodeling in the right proportions. The yodel, which is almost unique to western music here in America, adds a potency to this particular art form, which is seldom to never equaled elsewhere in the world of music. Of course, I may be a tad prejudiced, but, dad gummit, I challenge anybody to stand flat-footed without electricity and equal the power and beauty of a good western singer singing a "$Y^2$" song.

You know the yodel almost died out entirely a few years back. You just didn't hear it anywhere. It seemed doomed to appear only in a few halfhearted attempts by a handful of country singers. Now a halfhearted yodel can be likened to the old red steer—he tries so hard but just doesn't have the equipment to get the job done. Fortunately, I'm hearing a lot better yodeling these days. It's such a pleasure to hear a good yodeier hitting the high and low notes right on the numbers, and not only that, but they know how to speak the "lingo" of yodeling. These vocal techniques are the basis for tuning what might be considered vocal acrobatics into the spiritual communication I spoke of earlier. Yodeling at its best is not a horse race, but rather a pure expression of human spirit unhindered by language. The best of today's yodelers who, with great reverence speak of the old masters, also, in my opinion, owe them no apologies. When you couple this fresh talent with the songwriting of Ranger Doug or R. W. Hampton (some of the northern cowboys are up there, too) it starts to get plumb thrilling.

We can now hear and see the old classic done in grand fashion and ride new unfenced ranges as well. The West is not dead . . . I know, I live here, and it's a brand new day. Certainly the women are prettier, the horses are faster and smarter, there are more cattle on the range. Better get with it or you'll miss out. As for me, I can't wait to hear more. Keep a yodel in your heart and your pony 'tween his reins, and I'll be seeing you down the trail.

(Reprinted with permission from *The Sons of the Pioneers Historical Society Journal*, Volume 3, Number 1, Issue 8)

Canadian singer Wilf "Montana Slim" Carter influenced many yodelers from the late 1930s to the present.

## A RECENT HISTORY OF COWBOY AND WESTERN MUSIC
*William Jacobson*

The year 1987 marked a turning point for cowboy/western music. That year found the public's appreciation of the cowboy arts continuing to increase. Cody, Wyoming, held the fifth Cowboy Songs and Range Ballads weekend at the Buffalo Bill Historical Center, and Elko, Nevada, hosted its third Cowboy Poetry Gathering. Inspired by the Elko gatherings, Michael Martin Murphey hosted his first WestFest jamboree at Copper Mountain, Colorado. Riders in the Sky's eighth album, *The Cowboy Way* (MCA, 1987), was the first major label cowboy/western release since Rex Allen, Jr.'s, singing cowboy tribute, *Ridin' High* (Warner Brothers, 1982). Sons of the Pioneers historian Ken Griffis began publishing *The Sons of the Pioneers Historical Society Journal* in 1987. Because of a suggestion from western music fan Jim Martin in the pages of that newsletter, in 1988, retired real-estate developer and music patron Bill Wiley threw a western-music festival in Las Vegas. The Western Music Association and its associated November festival in Tucson were an outgrowth of this event. In 1988, cowboy humorist Baxter Black released his seventh volume of cowboy poetry, *Croutons on a Cowpie.*

In 1990, Michael Martin Murphey, Don Edwards, Sons of the San Joaquin, Suzy Bogguss, and western painter William Matthews appeared on The Nashville Network's *Nashville Now* to promote Murphey's upcoming *Cowboy Songs* album (Warner Brothers, 1990). This broadcast reportedly had the largest audience ever. Also in 1990, the first issue of *Song of the West* (formerly *The Sons of the Pioneers Historical Society Journal*) was published, which chronicled events in the cowboy/western music world, and Darrell Arnold, an advocate of cowboy and western music, left his position at *Western Horseman* to start his own publication, *Cowboy Magazine.* A number of slick western lifestyle magazines eventually followed suit as the cowboy image regained its popularity.

By this time, cowboy poetry gatherings were popping up all over the West, including Wickenburg, Flagstaff, Prescott, and Phoenix, Arizona; Carson City, Nevada; Alpine, Lubbock, and Abilene, Texas; Pendleton, Oregon; Oklahoma City, Oklahoma; Medora, North Dakota; Rapid City, South Dakota; Salinas and Bishop, California; Lehi and Tremonton, Utah; Silver City, New Mexico; Riverton, Wyoming; and Durango, Arvada, State Bridge, Colorado Springs, La Veta, and Steamboat Springs, Colorado.

The media became attracted to these stirrings in the West, and the general public had an increased awareness of things cowboy and western. Cheaply made television Westerns were produced, as well as western television specials, which often featured country singers who apparently were hoping to revive fading careers. Most importantly, though, good cowboy and western acts were finally heard outside the folklorist and tourist ghettos.

As the current cowboy fad wears out, there will probably be a decrease of interest in things western, including the music. At worst, the music, as well as other cowboy arts, will retreat to the fans, folklorists, musicians, and cowboys who always loved it. Through its strengths, cowboy/western will remain an essential American art form, just as bluegrass, blues, jazz, and Appalachian folk music have survived temporary surges in popularity. To quote Ian Tyson, "You know the West ain't never gonna die."

## DARRELL ARNOLD
*Born in LaVeta, Colorado, July 14, 1946*

*Cowboy Magazine* publisher/editor and former *Western Horseman* editor, Arnold has had some of his poems set to music by such cowboy musicians as Jack Hannah (the Sons of the San Joaquin), Ed Stabler, and Fletcher Jowers. A central figure, Darrell can often be found at various western gatherings and events. A volume of his poetry, *Cowboy Poultry Gatherin'*, was published in 1993 by Guy Logsdon Books.

A strong supporter of cowboy and western music, the amiable Darrell Arnold remarks, "I publish *Cowboy Magazine*, which includes stories on contemporary western singers as well as reviews of cowboy and western albums. I do all I can to encourage people to buy western and cowboy rather than country albums."

**Darrell Arnold. (*Song of the West* collection.)**

# THE HAYS COUNTY GALS

*Born in Austin, Texas, August 29, 1951—*
*Ginger Evans.*
*Born in Dallas, Texas, May 12, 1949—*
*Michael Fowler.*
*Born in Austin, Texas, July 7, 1951—Jill Jones.*
*Born in Oklahoma City, Oklahoma, June 9,*
*1947—Greg Lowry.*
*Born in Texarkana, Texas, September 23,*
*1948—Joan Rothelle*

The Hays County Gals present a blend of music, comical skits, and historical facts, focusing on the old-time cowboy and his lifestyle. With the help of props, costumes, and special effects, they create a feel for the Old West. Many of their songs are familiar classics.

**Hays County**
**Gals. (*Song of the West* collection.)**

The Hays County Gals came together as neighbors and friends to create a special show for their children's schools during the Texas sesquicentennial celebrations of 1986. What followed were requests for repeat performances at other schools in the area. As the Gals continued to study the era and search for more songs, they became increasingly intrigued by the history and the songs of cowboys, and worked them into a short, educational program for school children and into a full-length program for those of all ages.

The Hays County Gals sing three-part harmony, and do some yodeling in harmony. Jill plays guitar, Ginger, the standup bass, and Joanne, the fiddle. For the last two years, they have had a couple of sidekicks, Mike Fowler on the fiddle and Greg Lowry on dobro, mandolin, and accordion.

# BAXTER BLACK

*Born January 10, 1945*

Baxter Black is the nation's most popular cowboy poet/humorist and also a contemporary cowboy songwriter who has had songs recorded by Red Steagall, Ed Bruce, Pinto Bennett, and Fletcher Jowers. Ian Tyson collaborated with him on "Chasin' the Moon," which is on Tyson's *Eighteen Inches of Rain.* In addition to making over one hundred personal appearances each year and writing songs, Black writes a weekly newspaper column, is heard on National Public Radio, produces a short weekly radio series "Baxter on Monday," and is a novelist.

He grew up in Las Cruces, New Mexico, and attended New Mexico State University before earning his veterinarian degree at Colorado State University. He worked for the Diamond A Cattle Company and the Simplot Livestock Company before becoming a full-time entertainer and head cowboy of the Coyote Cowboy Company in Brighton, Colorado.

**Photo taken during the filming of *Baxter Black's 1st Video*. Baxter Black (background) with Too Slim in South Platte River. (*Song of the West* collection. Photo by Mary Rogers.)**

**Lanny Fiel. (*Song of the West* collection.)**

## LANNY FIEL
*Born in Dallas, Texas, June 10, 1950*

Lanny Fiel is responsible for producing many fine projects out of Lubbock, Texas. In 1991 and 1992 alone, Fiel produced albums by Joe Stephenson, R. W. Hampton, Leon Flick, and Jason Jones, as well as Buck Ramsey's *Rolling Uphill From Texas*, which won a 1992 Western Heritage Award. Not only a producer, Lanny plays mandolin, fiddle, harmonica, guitar, piano, and sings harmony vocals. He is the author of two western-swing music books, *Play It Lazy; the Bob Wills Fiddle Legacy* with Frankie McWhorter (Texas Tech University Press, 1992) and *The Essential Texas Fiddle; Improvisation, Harmony and Style* (Texas Tech University Press and Mel Bay Publications, 1992).

**Trivia: Lanny Fiel currently plays viola with the Lubbock Symphony Orchestra.**

## PINTO BENNETT, "THE FAMOUS MOTEL COWBOY"
*Born in Ames, Iowa, May 20, 1948*

This western singer/songwriter is better known in Europe than in his own country, and his recordings are easier to find there than in the United States. He has played to "sold out" audiences throughout Europe and to small honky-tonk patrons in the West. Bennett grew up on his grandfather's sheep ranch near Bennett, Idaho, and learned to play the guitar in "self defense." He played in local dance halls and in a variety of touring bands before organizing his Famous Motel Cowboy Band. He tried his contemporary cowboy/western music at Nashville before returning to Idaho.

**Pinto Bennett the famous "Motel Cowboy." Guy (Photo by Jim Schafer, Fort Collins, Colorado.)**

**Fletcher Jowers.**

# FLETCHER JOWERS
*Born in Kilgore, Texas, August 13, 1944*

A cowboy singer from Texas, Fletcher Jowers grew up with cowboy music and cowboying along with Hollywood's images of the singing cowboy. Over his life, Fletcher has cowboyed, done military service in Vietnam, been a railroad engineer, and has driven an eighteen-wheeler, hauling burros and goats between Texas and California. His recordings are mostly older cowboy material. His releases include *Songs of A Texas Cowboy* (1991) and *Sing Me A Cowboy Song* (1992).

# JOHNNY BAKER
*Birth information not found*

L ittle is known about Johnny Baker, who wrote and recorded rodeo songs in the 1960s and 1970s. His album titles are *Songs of the Rodeo, Let 'er Buck, Rodeo in the Sky, Rodeoin' with Johnny Baker,* and possibly other albums. He was the first genuine rodeo cowboy to write and record a series of songs about rodeo life. He produced and marketed his own recordings with an address in Edwards, Missouri.

# TOM RUSSELL
*Born in Yuma, Arizona, March 5, 1952*

T om Russell's life has been a colorful one. He has roamed from Los Angeles, Nigeria, Vancouver, Texas, Puerto Rico, to New York, drifting, writing, and singing. After a chance meeting with The Grateful Dead's Robert Hunter, Tom wound up on stage at New York's Bottom Line, singing his classic song "Gallo del Cielo."

Russell has combined talents with Ian Tyson on songwriting, most notably "Navajo Rug" and "Claude Dallas." In 1992, Russell's *Cowboy Real* album was released—all acoustic, with minimal instrumentation accompanying him. A balladeer of gutsy cowboy songs with few peers, it is hoped Tom Russell will continue to release material in this vein.

**Tom Russell. (Photograph by David Gahr.)**

83

## DON EDWARDS
*Born in Boonton, New Jersey, March 20, 1939*

Don Edwards is recognized as one of the finest interpreters of cowboy and western music. In the past, his classic western voice was likened to Marty Robbins's voice, but he has developed his own blues-influenced cowboy singing style as well as his own western swing voice.

Like many boys, young Don Edwards idolized the cowboy way of life. He would religiously listen to Gene Autry every Sunday night on the radio. After growing up with the West on his mind, he moved to Texas in the winter of 1958. He worked as a cowboy singer at the Six Flags Over Texas amusement park from 1960 to 1964 and made his first recording, a forty-five single named "The Young Ranger" at the end of his stay there. Don Edwards later made a name for himself in the Fort Worth area performing in the stockyards' White Elephant Saloon, where he still performs four times a year.

Many cowboy music fans have found Edwards's innovative work to be of superior quality, well-researched and modestly recorded, which gives a more traditional feel to the material. His *Happy Cowboy* album (1980) celebrated the legacy of Hollywood's singing cowboys. Two of his releases, *Songs of the Cowboy* (1986) and *Guitars and Saddle Songs* (1987), came with small songbooks to be read while listening. A scholar of cowboy song, Edwards intended these books to resemble N. Howard "Jack" Thorp's classic *Songs of the Cowboys* collection. Not one to continually repeat himself, Don moved on to release a western swing-flavored album, *Desert Nights and Cowtown Blues*, which was *Song of the West* magazine readers' favorite release for 1990. The following year, his excellent *Chant of the Wanderer* won the Western Heritage Wrangler Award for outstanding traditional cowboy/western music. After re-releasing five self-produced albums on his own Seven Shoux label, the independent-minded Edwards was one of the first artists signed to the Warner Western label. His first release for Warner Western, *Songs of the Trail* (1992), topped the *Song of the West* readers' poll for that year. In 1993, Warner Western released his outstanding *Goin' Back To Texas*.

Don Edwards has been seen on television's *Nashville Now, Austin City Limits, Texas Connection,* and many other shows, adding a real cowboy flair to otherwise stock country programming. A singer in constant demand, he has lent his talents to Michael Martin Murphey (*Cowboy Songs* and *Cowboy Christmas*), Nanci Griffith (*Other Voices, Other Rooms*), Tommy Morrell (*How the West Was Swung*), and *The Wild West* television miniseries soundtrack. He has also added his warm, friendly voice and music to films for the American Quarter Horse Association Museum and the Department of the Interior National Park Service, as well as numerous television miniseries and specials.

Edwards and his wife Kathy can be seen at many cowboy/western events across the West. An immensely talented and charming individual, Don Edwards is *the* cowboy balladeer for our time.

## CHRIS LEDOUX
*Born in Biloxi, Mississippi, October 2, 1948*

Chris LeDoux is a rodeo cowboy turned cowboy singer, with one boot firmly in rock and roll and the other in country music. He picked up his guitar on the rodeo circuit and began playing and writing songs. Because of his reputation for his rodeo songs, he began to record them and develop a family business, American Cowboy Songs, run by his father, Al LeDoux.

While releasing over twenty self-made albums, LeDoux continued to rodeo, and his career peaked after winning the 1976 world championship in bareback riding. He finally quit in 1984 to work full-time on his music career. In 1991, he signed a major label deal with Capitol, signifying that his following had far outgrown his tape distribution of rodeos, tack stores, and truck stops. An association with Garth Brooks on "Whatcha Gonna Do with a

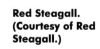

Chris LeDoux. (Photograph by Butch Adams.)

Cowboy" drew him closer to the public eye. His most popular early material may be found on *Radio and Rodeo Hits* (American Cowboy Songs, 1990).

# RED STEAGALL
*Born in Gainesville, Texas, December 22, 1938*

At age fifteen, Red Steagall fought against all odds when he contracted polio and spent months training his left hand to play guitar chords. Western swing music was always a part of his life. While playing and singing at night, he graduated from West Texas State University with a degree in Animal Science and Agronomy. After working in the field of Agricultural Chemistry, he spent eight years as a music industry executive in Hollywood. He now plies his trade as a recording artist, songwriter, poet, and television and motion-picture personality.

Steagall is well known in music circles for his Texas-style western swing music, but he is equally respected for his cowboy songs, ballads, and poetry. His hits have included "Here We Go Again," "Texas Red," "Party Dolls and Wine," "Freckles Brown," and that Texas classic, "Lone Star Beer and Bob Wills Music." His songwriting credits also include the theme for the National Finals Rodeo telecast and songs in *Vanishing Point, Drive-In, Shadows on the Wall, Savannah Smiles,* and *Dark Before Dawn.*

Steagall has performed at major rodeos, toured Europe, the Middle East, and South America, and has worked as a television host and a movie producer (*Big Bad John*). He was part of the first Elko Cowboy Poetry Gathering and is on the Western Folklife Center's National Advisory Council. In January 1991, he missed the Elko gathering in order to recite "The Cowboy's Prayer" for President and Mrs. Bush and representatives of 140 nations. In April 1991, the Texas Legislature named Red Steagall as the official Cowboy Poet of Texas.

Some of the albums Steagall has recorded include *Cowboy Favorites* for Delta, *Party Dolls and Wine* for Capitol, *Lone Star Beer and Bob Wills Music,* and *For All Our Cowboy Friends* for ABC (now MCA), and *Ride for the Brand* and *Nothin' But a Cowboy* for his own RS Records. In 1992, Red signed to record his cowboy music and poetry for the Warner Western label, and *Born to this Land* was his first Warner release. His earlier albums feature his vivid cowboy poetry; *Ride for the Brand* is all poetry. Both his poetry and songs often deal with the harsh reality of cowboying; pain and death are not excluded in his work. Red Steagall is well loved by the traditional rodeo crowd, cowboy poetry audiences, and, most of all, western swing dancers.

Red Steagall. (Courtesy of Red Steagall.)

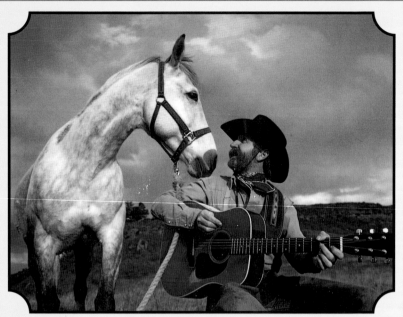

**Gary McMahan serenading his horse. (Photograph by Mary Rogers.)**

## GARY MCMAHAN

*Born in Greeley, Colorado, August 28, 1948*

Gary McMahan is a westerner who is equal parts cowboy singer, songwriter, poet, storyteller, and yodeler. With a rich heritage of farmers, ranchers, and stockmen from both sides of his family tree, his lyrics are more genuine than those of most western singers. His yodeling ability is among the best of contemporary performers.

McMahan has made his living working with horses and cattle and performing cowboy music. He has entertained around campfires, gatherings, conventions, and even on a backcountry packing trip with Ivana Trump and her children. One of the participants of Elko's first Cowboy Poetry Gathering, he, along with Ian Tyson, is acknowledged as one of the pioneers of contemporary cowboy music. "The First Cowboy Song," written by McMahan and Douglas B. Green, won a National Cowboy Hall of Fame Western Heritage award for best original cowboy song of 1992. His classic "Old Double Diamond" has been recorded by Ian Tyson, Chris LeDoux, Horse Sense, and countless other artists. Riders in the Sky recorded his "Ol' Cowpoke" on their *Cowboy Jubilee* album.

McMahan's albums include *Colorado Blue* (Tomato Records, 1980), *Saddle 'Em Up and Go!* (Horse Apple Records, 1988), and *A Cowboyin' Day* (Horse Apple Records, 1992), which contains his epic poem of the same name.

## GIL PRATHER

*Born in Abilene, Texas, July 10, 1940*

Gil Prather is a fourth-generation Texan who writes cowboy songs, often involving personal relationships. His expressive voice is one of the most distinctive in contemporary cowboy/western music.

Like many young west Texas cowboys, Gil Prather participated in rodeo. Family ranching interests and rodeo drew Prather to Alpine, Texas, where he attended Sul Ross State University and then ranched in the Big Bend region. He also cowboyed in the Rio Grande region, which had a major influence on his singing and songwriting.

Prather's single, "Santa Anna"/"Keep Me" (Sims, 1968), was a hit across the border of Texas. His album releases include *Back on the Border* (Cowboy Connection, 1990) and *Saddle Up and Bring Your Dreams Along* (Cowboy Connection, 1994).

**Gil Prather. (*Song of the West* collection.)**

# MICHAEL MARTIN MURPHEY

*Born in Dallas, Texas, March 14, 1946*

**M**ichael Martin Murphey is an engaging western entertainer with a winsome voice and a strong rhythm guitar style. He has successfully promoted many other artists on his WestFest shows, his television appearances, and his own cowboy music albums. Murphey began serenading as a professional at the Sky Ranch in Texas, performing old-time cowboy songs for guests there. From 1964 to 1970, he was a staff songwriter for Screen Gems, producing themes and songs for television. He formed Lewis and Clark Expedition, releasing one album in 1971; then he went solo.

Murphey moved to Austin, Texas, and was aligned with the "Outlaw" movement in country music that was emerging at the time. After signing up with A & M, he had a top-forty song "Geronimo's Cadillac," which developed into an American Indian rights anthem. In 1975, he saw a number-three single with "Wildfire." Then a duet with John Denver, "Mansion On A Hill," was his debut on the country charts. In the 1980s, Murphey had several country hits.

At an Elko Cowboy Poetry Gathering, Murphey was struck by the quality of the poetry and music as well as the camaraderie among performers there. Because of his admiration of Buffalo Bill, he began hosting an annual series of outdoor extravaganzas called WestFests at Copper Mountain, Colorado, and other western locations. These festivals feature cowboy, American Indian, western and country music, arts, crafts, and food.

Murphey's move to his Riverside Ranch near Taos, New Mexico, kept him closer to cowboy culture. He argued with his record label, Warner Brothers, to allow him to release a cowboy music album. After months of deliberation, Warner's Jim Ed Norman gave him the okay, warning him he was probably committing commercial suicide.

Murphey's 1990 album *Cowboy Songs* found him returning to his cowboy roots. The winner of a special National Cowboy Hall of Fame Wrangler award for preserving the cowboy music art form, it is Murphey's best-selling album to date. Because of the success of *Cowboy Songs*, Murphey persuaded Jim Ed Norman and Warner Brothers to create a major recording label for cowboy and western music, Warner Western. Murphey has subsequently released *Cowboy Songs II: Cowboy Christmas* and *Cowboy Songs III: Rhymes of the Renegades*.

**Trivia: Murphey's songs have been recorded by Hoyt Axton, Bill Miller, Cher, John Denver, Michael Nesmith, Sons of the San Joaquin, and the Monkees.**

**Michael Martin Murphey.
(Photograph by Mary Murphey.)**

**Ed Stabler. (*Song of the West* collection.)**

# ED STABLER

*Born in Macon, Georgia, July 26, 1942*

Ed Stabler is a contemporary cowboy folk singer/songwriter known for his immaculate finger-picking style and impeccable vocal diction.

His family moved to a small ranch near Colorado Springs, Colorado, when he was five years old. A gift guitar on his tenth birthday started him off into a variety of music forms. He sang songs in the heyday of folk clubs and coffeehouses in the 1960s and has worked before a microphone in radio and as a news anchorman in television. The reemergence of cowboy music in the 1980s and 1990s found Ed joining in with the music he has always loved. He often performs classic poems that he has set to music. His self-released cassette albums include *Ponies* (1990), *His Knibbs and the Badger* (with Katie Lee, 1992), and *Partner of the Wind* (Topplerock, 1993). Today, he ranches in Craig, Colorado, with his wife, Mary.

# IAN TYSON

*Born in Victoria, British Columbia, Canada, September 25, 1933*

Ian Tyson has experienced two musical careers in his lifetime. The first was in the folk music boom of the early 1960s, and these days he has been reborn, so to speak, as the undisputed premier contemporary cowboy singer/songwriter.

Raised on a farm in Canada, Tyson was brought up on Will James's books and the powerful image of the cowboy and the cowboy life. In high school, he rodeoed and later worked logging and construction jobs. Seriously injured while rodeoing at age nineteen, he taught himself guitar during his long convalescence.

Enrolling in the Vancouver School of Art at age twenty-one, Tyson found time to sing and dip his cowboy boots in the world of music. In 1958, he hitchhiked to Toronto after graduating. Tyson found employment as a commercial artist during the day and entered the budding folk club scene at night. This is where he met Sylvia Fricker, and they began singing together in 1959.

Ian and Sylvia, as the duo was known, had their first United States concert in 1961, then moved to New York and obtained a recording contract with Vanguard Records and Albert Grossman. In 1962, their debut album, *Ian and Sylvia*, stressed traditional folk tunes sung in a unique, uncompromising way. By 1964, they had released their second album and were married. Their music was a mixture of folk, cowboy, and pop influences. Without having huge chart toppers themselves, Tyson's "Four Strong Winds" was a 1965 country hit for Bobby Bare, and Judy Collins recorded his "Someday Soon" with success. Peaking in the mid-1960s as a folk act, in the latter 1960s Ian and Sylvia moved on to country music and the city of Nashville. The "country rock" created by them at this time failed to gain the complete support of the Nashville establishment. Tyson then wrote "Summer Wages" and other western songs, moving him into more of a cowboy frame of mind and reminding him of his unforgotten background.

They toured with their road band called Great Speckled Bird with unsuccessful reception from both country and folk fans.

Tyson was busted in 1972 for marijuana possession, and the duo was unable to tour in the United States for ten years, further stalling their musical careers. Moving back to Canada, they cohosted a weekly television show, *Nashville North,* which turned into *The Ian Tyson Show* when the couple divorced in 1975.

During his music career, Tyson took the opportunity to keep in touch with the cowboy side of himself, working, training, and riding horses in his off-time. In 1978, fellow Canadian and rock-and-roll legend Neil Young put out his return-to-folk album *Comes A Time* (Reprise, 1978). Included in this huge seller was Tyson's "Four Strong Winds." This was a turning point for Tyson, because he was able to return to the West and buy a ranch in the foothills of the Alberta Rockies with the help of royalty money he earned from Young's recording. He could now concentrate on ranching, cutting horses, and writing songs. He picked up a band to play occasionally in bars in the area, but that atmosphere wasn't to his liking. Later, with encouragement, Tyson's western songs were met with enthusiastic response when he was pursued to perform to a more cowboy and western audience. Thus was the beginning of his "cowboy culture" albums. The first was recorded in his bunkhouse, *Old Corrals and Sagebrush*. His *Cowboyography* album, with its elaborate production, was a commercial turning point in Canada. His "cowboy culture" albums are considered authoritative with their wealth of old cowboy favorites arranged Tyson style and new cowboy classics such as "Will James," "The Gift," "Fifty Years Ago," "Cowboys Don't Cry," and "Jaquima To Freno" (with Blaine McIntyre). The accolades for his work have come in the form of gold records and numerous industry awards.

Ian Tyson's experience as a highly crafted songwriter and his good ear for song arrangement are what really set him off from the hundreds of "sure 'nuff" cowboys who strap on a guitar. Working cowboys know if you are the real thing by your walk, your talk, and the way you wear your hat. Ian's material comes out of his genuine experiences and know-how as a cowboy. This is part of the reason he is ardently embraced by folks who know exactly what he is saying in the lyrics—something Hollywood could never manufacture—the real West.

Tyson's studio work and live work take traditional cowboy instrumentation into the modern age. The songs are cowboy through and through, but one can expect electric guitar, steel guitar, electronic keyboards, full drums, along with Tyson strumming on an acoustic and a fiddle and bass player. He isn't locked into conventions in order to

tell us a story in his songs, and the power and versatility in this method works beautifully.

If Tyson isn't touring and singing out in the West, he can be found in his Alberta home raising and training his beloved cutting horses or sweating out a new cowboy classic in his remote log cabin.

**TRIVIA:**

**Ian and Sylvia's first album was recorded in the Masonic Temple in Brooklyn, New York.**

**Tyson's "Someday Soon" was a top-ten country hit for Suzy Bogguss in 1991.**

**Ian Tyson and Big John. (Photograph by Gordon Biblow.)**

# TRADITIONAL COWBOY (FOLK)

## FOLK VARIETY
### FV 12001

CARL T. SPRAGUE
THE FIRST POPULAR SINGING COWBOY

**Carl T. Sprague's Folk Variety album *The First Popular Singing Cowboy*, 1972. (Courtesy of Richard Weize.)**

## CARL T. SPRAGUE

*Born near Houston, Texas, in 1895*

Music historian John I. White gave Carl T. Sprague the label "The Original Singing Cowboy." A more accurate description appeared on the cover of the 1972 album *Carl T. Sprague: The First Popular Singing Cowboy* Folk Variety (FV 12001). He wasn't the first, but he was the first popular cowboy singer. During his initial session for Victor records in Camden, New Jersey, August 1925, he recorded ten songs, including D. J. O'Malley's "When the Work's All Done This Fall," which reportedly has sold 900,000 copies, an amazing number of sales for that time period.

Sprague was born into a cattle-raising family, often claiming that he learned many of his songs from working cowboys. In 1915, he enrolled at Texas A & M, where he expanded his musical skills. After a stint in military service during World War I, he returned to A & M, graduating in 1922. He remained there in the athletic department for the next fifteen years.

Sprague was inspired by the success of Vernon Dalhart to record his songs. While he did not enjoy the same widespread popularity, he did leave a legacy of cowboy songs, recorded during four sessions between 1925 and 1929. His last recording session was for Richard Weize and the Folk Variety Label (Germany) in 1972.

During his lifetime, he worked at a wide variety of occupations, living most of the time in the Bryan, Texas, area.

## ALEXANDER CAMPBELL "ECK" ROBERTSON

*Born in Delaney, Arkansas, November 20, 1887*

Alexander Campbell "Eck" Robertson was the first musician to record a country/western tune for a commercial recording company, and he played a major role in the development of the fiddling style known as "Texas-Oklahoma Fiddling." He and Henry C. Gilliland from Altus, Oklahoma, traveled to New York City, where they recorded "Arkansas Traveler" and "Turkey in the Straw" for the Victor Talking Machine Company, June 30, 1922. Gilliland played second fiddle to Robertson's lead fiddle.

Robertson grew up part of an Arkansas farm family who were traditional fiddlers, so he started fiddling at an early age. When he was sixteen, he decided to leave home to make his living as a musician. He made his way into Indian Territory (Oklahoma), moving from ranch to ranch. Eventually he went to work for a medicine show that traveled throughout Indian Territory. He became a showman known as the "cowboy fiddler." "Uncle John" Wills (the father of Bob Wills)

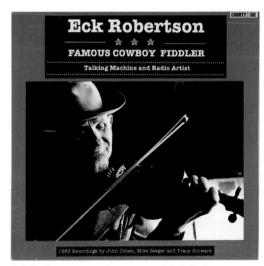

**Eck Robertson on the cover of *Eck Robertson: Famous Cowboy Fiddler,* 1991. (Courtesy of County Records.)**

90

and he competed against each other in fiddling contests in the Texas Panhandle, where he made his home in the 1920s.

The best example of Robertson's fiddling is *Eck Robertson: Famous Cowboy Fiddler* issued by County Records in 1991. This collection was recorded by John Cohen, Mike Seeger, and Tracy Schwarz (The New Lost City Ramblers) in 1963.

Robertson died February 15, 1975.

## JULES VERNE ALLEN
*Born in Waxahachie, Texas, April 1, 1883*

Little is known about this cowboy singer other than his autobiographical sketch from *Cowboy Lore* (San Antonio: Naylor Printing Co., 1933) He said that he started working cattle in Texas at the age of ten and was a horse wrangler—the lowest position in cow camps—five times on cattle drives to Montana.

Along the way, he learned to play the guitar and picked up a few songs. He volunteered for service in World War I and apparently worked as a cow-hand in rodeos and as a police officer during the 1920s. With the growth of radio popularity and cowboy music, he became a radio performer and claimed to be "The Original Singing Cowboy." His appearances included KNX and WFI, Los Angeles; WFAA, Dallas; and WOAI and KTSA, San Antonio.

In San Antonio his shows were sponsored by the Longhorn Portland Cement Company; they published a small songbook, *Cowboy Songs Sung by Longhorn Luke and His Cowboys* (date unknown), which is now extremely rare. The size of his band and the members remaining are unknown. On April 21, 1928, he recorded three songs for RCA Victor in El Paso, where he lived at that time. His last session was April 29, 1929, in Culver City, California.

During six sessions, he recorded twenty-four sides, of which two can be heard on *Authentic Cowboys and Their Western Folksongs* (RCA Victor) and sixteen are on *Jules Verne Allen: The Texas Cowboy* (Folk Variety Records).

Jules Verne Allen died in 1945.

Jules Verne Allen on the cover of "The Rovin' Gambler" sheet music, 1935. (Guy Logsdon and the Ranch House Library.)

## ROBERT OWEN "BOB" ATCHER
*Born in Hardin County, Kentucky, May 11, 1914*

Bob Atcher specialized in American folk songs and cowboy songs and is remembered for his years on Chicago's WLS "National Barn Dance." He grew up in a musical family who left Kentucky in 1919 for North Dakota. There he learned cowboy songs that complemented his rich background in traditional southern music. The family returned to Kentucky following seven years of rugged Dakota life.

In the late 1920s, Atcher's radio career started in Louisville. By 1932 he had moved to Chicago, to Atlanta, and then to West Virginia, always working for radio stations.

Atcher returned to Chicago in 1938, continuing his radio work there. When Rex Allen left the "National Barn Dance" in 1950, WLS hired Atcher to replace him.

The YELLOW ROSE of TEXAS

with
UKELELE CHORDS
GUITAR CHORDS
and
SPECIAL HAWAIIAN
GUITAR CHORUS

BONNIE BLUE EYES
and
BOB ATCHER

CALUMET MUSIC CO.
201 EAST 26th STREET
CHICAGO, ILL.

V 1152

**Bob Atcher with Bonnie Blue Eyes on the cover of "The Yellow Rose of Texas" sheet music, 1935.**

Through most of Atcher's career, his singing partner was his wife, Leota Applegate, better known as Bonnie Blue Eyes.

Atcher recorded for Columbia and mixed country songs with cowboy songs. Acuff-Rose Publications published a Bob Atcher songbook in the 1940s, but it contained no cowboy songs. He remained a popular singer in the Chicago area for many, many years, and he also served as the mayor of Schaumburg, Illinois, a Chicago suburb, before returning to Kentucky.

Bob Atcher, once billed the "Dean of Cowboy Singers," died October 30, 1993, in Prospect, Kentucky.

## WILLIAM "BILL" BENDER, JR.
*Born in New York, August 1, 1916*

In the late 1930s, Bill Bender recorded cowboy/western songs for Elite, Varsity, and US labels. In the 1940s, Moses Asch copied the Varsity discs and issued *Frontier Ballads and Cowboy Songs* (Asch 410), and Herbert Harris took the Asch copies and issued the same songs under the

Stinson label. Bender apparently learned his songs from songbooks when cowboy songs were popular in the thirties, and sang them over a local radio station in White Plains, New York. He saw military service in World War II and the Korean War as a radio combat reporter. Bender sang with a pleasing baritone voice; unfortunately, little information about his life is known.

## GILBERT VANDINE "CISCO" HOUSTON
*Born in Wilmington, Delaware, August 18, 1918*

Cisco Houston sang and recorded cowboy, union, love, children, mining, and hundreds of other kinds of songs about life in the United States. In most of his recordings he sang harmony with Woody Guthrie, his friend and traveling companion. He had an ability to adjust his voice quality to blend with many vocal styles, but when he sang alone, Houston had a strong smooth voice, a voice better than most folk singers in the forties and fifties. His first long-playing record, issued by Folkways Records, was *Cowboy Songs* (FA 2022) in 1952, but he and Woody Guthrie had recorded cowboy songs as a duet as early as 1944.

Houston learned many cowboy/western songs traveling through the West, and he shared them with young folksingers. He was a quieter influence than Woody Guthrie or Leadbelly, but he did have an influence on many young singers of songs from the West in the fifties and sixties. Cisco Houston died of cancer, April 28, 1961.

## LEADBELLY
(BIRTHNAME—HUDDIE WILLIAM LEDBETTER)
*Born in Mooringsport, Louisiana, January 29, 1889*

Leadbelly was not a cowboy, but he recorded a few cowboy/western songs. More importantly, he was an influence in American music, particularly among those who play the twelve-string guitar and those who sing the blues, including the cowboy blues. He and Tex Ritter were friends, and he knew other cowboy singers. He was in and out of prisons in Texas and Louisiana until John A. Lomax discovered him; his knowledge of songs, songwriting ability, and singing earned him his freedom, and he went on to become one of the most important figures in Twentieth Century music. He died December 6, 1949, and left a musical legacy that continues to grow. For the Leadbelly story see Charles Wolfe and Kip Lornell's *The Life and Legend of Leadbelly*, 1992.

## CHARLES NABELL

*Birth information not found*

Charles Nabell recorded "The Letter from Home Sweet Home," "The Great Round Up," and "Utah Carl" on November 28, 1924, for Okeh Records in St. Louis, Missouri, a few months after Fiddlin' John Carson recorded "Dixie Cowboy." He also recorded three other songs that were apparently religious in content during that session and is often referred to as the first to record cowboy songs. He recorded twelve additional songs during two later sessions. Nothing about Nabell is known other than that he recorded cowboy songs in 1924. For his story about searching for Nabell, see Thomas S. Johnson, "The Ghost of Charles Nabell: Searching for the First Recorded Western Folk Singer," *JEMF Quarterly* (Fall/Winter 1985) 77/78: 134–36.

## CHARLES BADGER CLARK, JR.

*Born in Albia, Iowa, in 1883*

The son of a Methodist minister, Badger Clark was three months old when the family moved to a farm in the Dakota Territory and in 1898 moved to Deadwood, South Dakota. In 1904, Clark, in poor health and seeking a warmer, drier climate, traveled to Arizona, where he worked on a ranch near Tombstone. While in Arizona, he wrote "A Cowboy's Prayer," which has been used as an "anonymous" poem for nearly a century and has been set to music as well as recited. In 1908, he returned to South Dakota where he built a cabin in Custer State Park near Custer City, and lived there the rest of his life. He died in 1957, leaving many poems that have been set to music, including "High Chin Bob" and "A Border Affair (Spanish Is the Loving Tongue)," set to music by Billy Simon. His book *Sun and Saddle Leather*, a western classic that has been reprinted many times, is a collection of his poems.

Woody Guthrie holding the bass fiddle and the Junior Chamber of Commerce band, Pampa, Texas. (Photograph courtesy of Woody Guthrie Publications.)

## WOODROW WILSON "WOODY" GUTHRIE

*Born in Okemah, Oklahoma, July 14, 1912*

Woody Guthrie is known for his "Dust Bowl Ballads" and topical songs, but he also knew, sang, wrote, and recorded cowboy songs. His father left Texas in 1897 and went to Indian Territory as a cowboy, working on a ranch near present-day Okmulgee, Oklahoma. Woody grew up hearing stories about family ranches and cowboys in Texas. Tragedy tore the family apart and made it necessary for them to move to Pampa, Texas. It was there Woody experienced dust storms.

In 1937, he traveled to Los Angeles, where he and his cousin, Jack, had a radio show, and where he wrote the western swing classic "Oklahoma Hills." Jack recorded it a few years later. Woody also wrote songs like "Philadelphia Lawyer" and hundreds more about life in the Southwest and West, as well as social protest songs. Woody's influence on songwriters and singers is widespread and continuing; he was and is a major influence in American music. Woody died from Huntington's disease on October 3, 1967.

John White on the the cover of the songbook *Cowboy Songs,* published by the Pacific Coast Borax Company, 1934. (Guy Logsdon and the Ranch House Library.)

## HARRY K. "HAYWIRE MAC" McCLINTOCK

*Born In Knoxville, Tennessee, October 8, 1882*

One of the most colorful singer/songwriters in American music, McClintock wrote "The Big Rock Candy Mountain," "Hallelujah, I'm a Bum," and other hobo/western classics. He was the first to commercially record "Billy Venero," "Sweet Betsy from Pike," "The Old Chisholm Trail," "Good-bye Old Paint," "Get Along, Little Dogies," and possibly others. He traveled extensively as a hobo; worked at many occupations; sang at churches, hobo camps, and IWW strikes; led a cowboy orchestra; and was a radio personality. In 1925, he started his radio career on KFRC, San Francisco, with a children's show. McClintock died April 24, 1957.

## JOHN I. WHITE

*Birth information not found*

White was a collector, singer, and scholar of cowboy songs. His book *Get Along, Little Dogies: Songs and Songmakers of the American West* (Urbana: University of Illinois Press, 1975) is a collection of articles he wrote about the makers of the songs and is essential for any study of cowboy/western music. He became interested in cowboy songs while visiting an Arizona dude ranch in 1924. Later, he became a singer of cowboy songs and in a few years was hired to sing cowboy songs at WOR in New York City. Along the paved trail, he became "The Lonesome Cowboy" and compiled a song folio, *The Lonesome Cowboy: Songs of Plains and Hills,* published in 1929.

White recorded a few cowboy songs for ARC and in 1930 was hired to sing on the weekly network radio show "Death Valley Days," sponsored by Pacific Coast Borax Company. He was on this show for six years and in 1934 published another song folio, *Cowboy Songs as Sung by John White "The Lonesome Cowboy" in Death Valley Days.* The same script with different actors and a different singer, Charles Marshall, was aired from the West Coast, and the same song folio with Marshall's name as the "Singing Cowboy" and photograph was issued.

When White left the show, he devoted his attention to his map business and upon retirement in 1965, returned to writing about and performing the songs he loved. In 1973, he recorded seventeen songs available in cassette format, *John I. White Songs of the American West.* He died in 1992 at the age of ninety, and his collection is available for research at Utah State University, Logan, Utah.

## ROSALIE STRINGFELLOW SORRELS

*Born in 1933*

Sorrels is a singer, songwriter, and recording artist who has entertained folk-circuit audiences across the nation. She grew up in Idaho and Utah and at an early age learned songs from her relatives. Some of those songs she collected for her first album, *Folk Songs of Idaho and Utah* (Folkways Records, FH 5343, 1961).

As a divorced parent with five children to support, Sorrels turned to folk music for a living and has recorded over twenty albums of her songs, traditional songs, and women's rights songs.

# JACK H. "POWDER RIVER" AND KITTY LEE

*Birth information not found*

This couple was one of the most colorful duets in western music. They were the first to record the popular "Sierry Petes," written by Gail Gardner and set to music by Bill Simon, but Jack Lee claimed that he wrote it as well as other traditional cowboy songs such as "Powder River, Let'er Buck." However, he was not the only one to claim authorship of old songs, and he may have written some of them.

Little is known about their background other than that they appeared on the scene when cowboy songs grew popular, and by 1930, Jack was billed as "Montana's Cowboy Poet." He later compiled a few folios and books containing cowboy songs and poems.

Powder River Jack and Kitty Lee on the cover of the songbook *Songs of the Range,* published by the Chart Music Publishing House, Chicago, Illinois. (Guy Logsdon and the Ranch House Library.)

Nevada Slim. (Guy Logsdon and the Ranch House Library.)

# DALLAS "NEVADA SLIM" TURNER

*Born in Walla Walla, Washington, November 27, 1927*

Turner was the last Mexican-border radio station singing cowboy and pitchman. He is a songwriter, a singer, and an encyclopedia of cowboy popular culture. He grew up on a ranch near Burns, Oregon, retaining genuine cowboy traditions to support his musical interests.

His early introduction to cowboy songs came from his mother, and his inspiration to sing came from Jack "Powder River" Lee. Later, when he became fascinated with radio broadcasting, he heard Cowboy Slim Rinehart, who became his border radio friend and leader. Turner, with Rinehart's encouragement, eventually broadcast for all border stations, using different names, such as Cowboy Slim, Tex Vernon, Yodeling Slim Dallas, and at least a dozen other names.

Turner has written over a thousand songs, published ten song folios, and recorded for Rural Rhythm, Rich R-Tone, and other record companies. He does not make many personal appearances but did perform at the 1993 Cowboy Music

Gathering in Elko, Nevada, gaining a new generation of fans. He lives in Reno, Nevada, and still has a magnificent radio voice. For more information about Turner, see Guy Logsdon, *"The Whorehouse Bells Were Ringing" and Other Songs Cowboys Sing* (Urbana: University of Illinois Press, 1989), 18–21.

**Stan Howe. (*Song of the West* collection.)**

## STAN HOWE
*Born in Baker, Montana, December 29, 1942*

A contemporary western singer, Stan Howe has several cassettes on his own Cowtown label. He also produced his own songbook *Singing Cowboys, My Scrapbook of Favorite Cowboy Songs* (1992), written for the beginning guitarist/singer.

## TONY KRABER
*Birth information not found*

Kraber recorded an album of western songs, *The Old Chisholm Trail Songs of the American West*, for Keynote Recordings in the early 1940s. He was an easterner who sang many different occupational songs and was involved in the early years of the urban folk revival and social protest music in New York City, singing mostly in clubs and cabarets.

## GAIL I. GARDNER
*Born near Prescott, Arizona, in 1892*

Gardner was a legendary Arizona poet who wrote "Sierry Petes," one of the most popular traditional cowboy poems/songs. He and a cowboy friend were camped in the Sierra Prieta Mountains west of Prescott, when they decided to ride to town for relaxation. Whiskey Row was, indeed, a row of bars—some still survive—that they visited, and in 1917, while on a train headed for military service, he wrote about their trip and the possible consequences. A few years later, his Arizona cowboy friend, Bill Simon, set it to music, and it quickly spread throughout the West. It remains one of the most popular traditional cowboy songs. For more of his poetry and life story, see Gail I. Gardner, *Orejana Bull*, seventh edition (Prescott, Arizona: Sharlot Hall Museum Press, 1987).

Gail Gardner died at his home ranch November 23, 1988.

## DOMINICK JOHN "D. J." O'MALLEY
*Born in New York City, New York, April 30, 1867*

O'Malley penned a few of the lasting poems/songs that are traditional among cowboys, such as "D-2 Horse Wrangler (The Tenderfoot)," "A Cowboy's Death (Charlie Rutledge)," "A Busted Cowboy's Christmas," and "When the Work's All Done This Fall."

When O'Malley was a young child, his father died, and his mother married Charles White, who moved the family to Fort Sanders, Wyoming Territory, in 1876 and joined the Second Cavalry. (O'Malley used the name White for many years.) In 1877, the Second Cavalry moved into Montana,

## CARMEN "CURLEY" WILLIAM FLETCHER

*Born in San Francisco, California, September 22, 1892*

Curley Fletcher was a Nevada/California cowboy who wrote songs and poems that have become cowboy classics, including "Strawberry Roan," "The Castration of the Strawberry Roan," "The Open Ledger (Book)," "The Flying U Twister (Bad Brahma Bull)," "Wild Buckaroo," and many more.

He grew up around the Bishop, California, area and worked as a cowhand as well as a rodeo cowboy in the formative years of the sport. He wrote "Strawberry Roan" as a poem in 1914; the identity of the person who set it to music is unknown. He privately published two books of poetry and one song folio; see his *Song of the Sage*, with a preface by Hal Cannon (Salt Lake City, Utah: Gibbs Smith, Publisher, 1986). Fletcher died in 1954.

**Curley Fletcher. (Guy Logsdon and the Ranch House Library.)**

and the White family followed. Four years later, O'Malley's stepfather deserted the Army and the family, and D. J. had to find work. He became a young Montana cowhand and cowboyed during the growth of the Montana livestock industry.

During those years, he wrote poems to be sung to well-known melodies and submitted many of them to the Miles City *Stock Growers' Journal.* His fellow cowboys quickly made them a part of cowboy culture. O'Malley died March 6, 1943. For his story, see John I. White, *Git Along, Little Dogies* (Urbana: University of Illinois Press, 1975), 73–100.

## SLIM CRITCHLOW

*Birth information not found*

Little is known about Slim Critchlow other than soon after his birth in Pennsylvania, his family moved to Iowa and then to Utah. Around 1913, they moved to Oklahoma, finally making the trek to California in 1923.

After graduating from high school, Critchlow made his way to Idaho and worked as a cowhand, learning cowboy songs along the way and eventually landing in Salt Lake City, where he sang as a drifting cowboy for KDYL. He and two friends formed the Utah Buckaroos, broadcasting on KSL.

Critchlow and his wife moved to California in 1936, where he died October 31, 1969. He sang for many folk festivals in California in the 1960s, and shortly before his death, recorded *Slim Critchlow: Cowboy Songs "The Crooked Trail to Holbrook"* (Arhoolie 5007).

## CARL SANDBURG

*Born in Galesburg, Illinois, January 6, 1878*

Carl Sandburg is best known for his poetry and Abraham Lincoln biographies, but he also collected and sang folk songs, including cowboy songs. As he traveled the nation, he gathered the songs of the people because of his fascination with and respect for the diversity of cultures, language, and customs. He put his songs into *The American Songbag* (New York: Harcourt, Brace, 1927), and in 1947 recorded *Cowboy Songs and Negro Spirituals* (Decca A-356). In his book and on record he included the cowboy classic "Colorado Trail."

Sandburg was given the song by a doctor in Duluth, Minnesota, who had treated a cowhand in a local hospital. The cowboy had brought a load of horses to the town and was severely injured while doing a few stunt rides. As he recuperated, he sang for the other patients. One of his songs was the first verse and chorus of "Colorado Trail." A few years later, Lee Hays, bass singer for The Weavers, wrote the additional verses that are sung by Ian Tyson and others. The song is an example of the cowboy song process and the vision of Carl Sandburg.

**Poster for John A. Lomax concert. (Guy Logsdon and the Ranch House Library.)**

## JOHN A. LOMAX
# COWBOY SONGS AND BALLADS
## COLLEGE AUDITORIUM

Saturday, *April 4, 1925,* 8:00 P. M. - - - *Admission 25 Cents*

Tickets on Sale at Tiger Drug Store and by Members of the English Department

"The leader was a feller that came from Swenson's ranch,—
They called him Windy Billy from Little Deadman's Branch.
His rig was kinder keerless,—big spurs and high heeled boots;
He had the reputation that comes when fellers shoots."
—*The Cowboys' Christmas Ball.*

"Cloudy in the west and lookin' like rain;
Damned old slicker in the waggin again."
—*The Old Chisholm Trail.*

"Fred, you take my saddle; George, you take my bed;
And, Bill, you take my pistol after that I am dead,
And think of me kindly when you look upon them all,
For I'll not see my mother when work is done this fall."
—*When Work Is Done This Fall.*

"Sam Bass was born in Indiana, that was his native home,
And at the age of seventeen young Sam began to roam.
He first came out to Texas, a cowboy for to be—
A kinder hearted feller you seldom ever see."
—*Sam Bass.*

"Oh bury me not on the lone prairie
Where the wild coyotes will howl o'er me,
Where the rattlesnakes hiss and the crow flies free
O bury me not on the lone prairie."
—*The Dying Cowboy.*

John A. Lomax, Austin, Texas, author of *"Cowboy Songs and Ballads"* and *"Songs of the*
cowboy songs than any man alive. He is a

## JOHN AVERY LOMAX AND ALAN LOMAX
*Birth information not found*

John A. Lomax was a Texan who grew up hearing cowboys sing their songs, and in 1908, he received a grant to record them. His collecting efforts resulted in the best-known and most widely used cowboy songbook ever published, *Cowboy Songs and Other Frontier Ballads* (New York: Sturgis and Walton, 1910). It was reissued in 1916, and a revised and enlarged edition with assistance from his son Alan was published in 1938, available now in paperback edition. He also compiled *Songs of the Cattle Trail and Cow Camp,* which was more cowboy poetry than songs.

Later, Lomax discovered the legendary singer Leadbelly and became curator of the Folk Archives at the Library of Congress, where he continued to collect folksongs across the nation. His thousands of recordings are available in the Archives of Folk Culture, Library of Congress.

Alan Lomax started traveling with his father in the early 1930s and co-authored with him six collections of folksongs. While working at the Library of Congress, he recorded Woody Guthrie and did much in promoting this music. He was instrumental in starting radio shows that introduced traditional music to millions of listeners. In 1960, his compilation, *The Folk Songs of North America,* was published by Doubleday. He continues to teach, write, sing, and collect.

## "FIDDLING" JOHN CARSON
*Born in Fannin County, Georgia, March 23, 1868*

"Fiddling" John Carson is generally considered to be a major pioneer in country music though not identified with cowboy/western music. However, it was he who first recorded "When the Work's All Done This Fall" and who probably was the first ever to record a cowboy song. He recorded it for the Okeh label under the title "Dixie Cowboy," in Atlanta, Georgia, during March of 1924. His melody was different than the popular melody used by most singers, but the lyrics were definitely a variant of D. J. O'Malley's song.

Carson worked at a variety of occupations, including house painter, moonshiner, and elevator operator. He died in December of 1949.

**Trivia: "When the Work's All Done This Fall" was recorded by at least twenty-nine singers and bands between 1924 and 1939, making it by far the most popular cowboy song of that era.**

## BILLIE MAXWELL
*Birth information not found*

Billie Maxwell was the first female to commercially record a cowboy song. On February 7, 1929, she recorded "Billie Venero" for Victor Records in El Paso, Texas. She accompanied herself on the guitar, and a fiddle player, probably E. C. Maxwell, played his fiddle. On the same day, Victor recorded the White Mountain Orchestra, composed of E. C. Maxwell (fiddle), F. L. Maxwell and F. M. Maxwell (guitars), and Mrs. A. C. Warner (banjo). It is not known if Billie was daughter, wife, in-law, cousin, or actually one of that group.

On November 11, 1929, Victor recorded four more songs by Billie, "The Arizona Girl I Left Behind Me," "The Cowboy's Wife," "Where Your Sweetheart Waits For You, Jack," and "Haunted Hunter." Scholars and collectors have unsuccessfully searched for information about Billie Maxwell and the White Mountain Orchestra. She can be heard on *Authentic Cowboys and Their Western Folksongs* (RCA Victor).

## NATHAN HOWARD "JACK" THORP

*Born in New York City, New York, June 10, 1867*

Jack Thorp was the first known collector of cowboy songs, and the first to edit and publish a cowboy songbook, *Songs of the Cowboy* (Estancia, New Mexico: New Print Shop, 1908; the expanded 1921 edition was reprinted by the University of Nebraska Press). He wrote "Little Joe the Wrangler," "Chopo," and other cowboy songs and poems. As a young man, Thorp visited his brother's ranch in Nebraska and fell in love with the West and cowboy life, eventually making New Mexico his home. For his experiences, see Thorp's *Pardner of the Wind* (Caldwell, Idaho: Caxton Printers, 1941; reprinted by the University of Nebraska Press). He died June 4, 1940, in his New Mexico home.

## BUNKHOUSE ORCHESTRA

*Birth information not found*

This band was originally known as the Deseret String Band and still uses that title occasionally. They specialize in playing western fiddle tunes, cowboy songs, and old western country songs and melodies.

Current and past members of this Utah-based group include Hal Cannon, Tom Carter, Greg Schaub, Skip Gorman, Leonard Coulson, Mark Jardine, Stephen Jardine, Rich McClure, and Ron Kane. In addition to making personal appearances, they recorded *Old-Time Cowboy Songs*, edited by Hal Cannon (Salt Lake City: Peregrine Smith Books, 1988) and, as the Deseret String Band, issued at least two cassettes of old-time music.

## "SAWYER" TOM HAYDEN

*Born in Denver, Colorado, January 21, 1956*

"Sawyer" Tom Hayden can usually be found by the cowboy music stage at Elko, because he has been the musical coordinator of the Elko Cowboy Poetry Gathering since 1985. A personable singer and entertainer, Tom released a cassette in 1989, *At Home on the Range*.

The "Sawyer" part of his name comes from his logging and sawmill profession. Tom often performs with John Nielson, who retired from touring with Justin Bishop in Horse Sense.

**Sawyer Tom Hayden (center).
(Photograph by Valerie Ulyett.)**

**Jim Bob Tinsley.
(Photograph by Greg Grant.)**

## JIM BOB TINSLEY

*Born in Brevard, North Carolina, August 12, 1921*

The Mountain Dance and Folk Festival in Asheville, North Carolina, provided the backdrop for Jim Bob Tinsley's debut as a folksinger and musician at age thirteen. He has also worked as a cowboy in Arizona and Florida.

Tinsley performed for and sang an impromptu duet with Sir Winston Churchill during World War II at the 1943 Casablanca Conference. Later, he was a consultant for Michael Martin Murphey on his breakthrough *Cowboy Songs* album (Warner Brothers, 1989), as well as providing some backup vocals. Among the many awards Tinsley has accumulated are the Western Heritage Wrangler Award of outstanding contribution to western heritage through music (1982) and the Pioneer Award (1984) from the National Radio Heritage Association, Council Bluffs, Iowa. An author of many books, Tinsley's most important contributions to cowboy and western music are *He Was Singin' This Song* (University of Central Florida Press, 1981) and *For a Cowboy Has To Sing* (University of Central Florida Press, 1991). He has also recorded and released corresponding albums with the same titles.

**Katie Lee. (Photograph and color tinting by Mary Rogers.)**

> **F**olk music is written by folks, and not for money and not for praise, nor for anything, except just to celebrate an event or to tell a story or to get a point across."
>
> **Katie Lee**

## KATIE LEE
*Born in Tucson, Arizona, October 23, 1919*

**K**atie Lee possesses a beautiful yet dramatic singing voice and a Spanish-flavored guitar strum. She is considered by many to be one of the finest cowboy folk singers alive. She is an astute critic and historian; her book *Ten Thousand Goddam Cattle*, a well-researched and loving work, is a must for any western library.

Katie Lee grew up near the Mexican border in Tucson. Her first instrument was the ukulele, but a boyfriend coerced her into learning the guitar. She took a trip to Mexico in 1942 and learned Spanish rhythms on the guitar from mariachis. Katie bought a guitar, brought it home with her, and taught herself to sing in Spanish.

After graduating with a B.A. in drama from the University of Arizona, Katie Lee headed out to Hollywood to pursue her interests in music and acting. She had stage roles in the Pasadena

Playhouse and Geller Theater. On radio she was an actress/singer on NBC's "The Great Gildersleeve," "The Halls of Ivy," "The Railroad Hour," "One Man's Family," and "The Roy Rogers Show." In the motion picture industry Lee had numerous bit and speaking parts. Television shows that she worked on included *Armchair Detective* (CBS, 1949), *Fireside Theater* (NBC, 1950–51), and she was the folk music director for *The Helen Parrich Telephone Hour* (NBC, 1952).

Lee's good friend and mentor Burl Ives advised her to leave Hollywood and play in the nightclubs, where audiences could appreciate her folk-music background. She proceeded to play clubs and coffeehouses from 1954 to 1968, including appearances at The Streamliner (Chicago), The Blue Angel (New York), Downstairs at the Upstairs (New York), The Hungry I (San Francisco), The Troubadour (Hollywood), and more.

Lee fell in love with the beauty of the Colorado River, and when plans were announced to flood Glen Canyon to create Lake Powell, she wrote the words and music to an album's worth of songs. Folkways Records released her *Folks Songs and Poems of the Colorado River* in 1964. She continues to write melodies to the words of others, especially using the poetry of the late Charles "Badger" Clark and Henry Herbert Knibbs. Her signature song is James Grafton Rogers's "The Town of Old Delores," but she is also an excellent interpreter of Tim Henderson ("Maria Consuela") and Tom Russell ("Gallo del Cielo").

In 1976, after fifteen years of research, Lee's essential work of folklore research, *Ten Thousand Goddam Cattle: A History of the American Cowboy in Song, Story and Verse,* was published by Northland Press. It was revised and released in 1985 by Katydid Books & Music. With the musical and vocal aid of David Holt, Travis Edmondson, and Earl Edmondson, she released a companion double-length album in 1976, which is highly recommended to those wishing a musical introduction to Katie Lee.

Lee's album work also includes *Spicy Songs of Cool Knight* (Specialty Records, 1956), *Song of Couch and Consultation* (Commentary Records, 1957), *Life Is Just a Bed of Neuroses* (RCA, 1959), *The Best of Katie Lee Live at the Troubadour* (Horizon Records, 1966), *Love's Little Sisters* (Katydid Records, 1975), *Ten Thousand Goddam Cattle* (Katydid Books & Records, 1976), *Fenced!* (Katydid Books & Records, 1983), *Colorado River Songs* (with re-recorded additions and deletions from the old Folkways recording, Katydid Books & Records, 1988), *His Knibbs and The Badger* (with Ed Stabler, Katydid Books & Records, 1992). She wrote and directed a documentary, *The Last Wagon* (Katydid Books & Records, 1971), which was produced originally for PBS and won the 1972 Golden Eagle Award from the Council of International Nontheatrical Events (CINE). This film features the cowboy songs, melodies, and poems of Gail Gardner, Billy Simon, and Katie Lee.

A cowboy singer of the true West, Katie Lee is in a field with few peers.

## RAYMOND (RAY) W. REED

*Born in San Jon, New Mexico, April 18, 1916*

Ray Reed grew up cowboying, rodeoing, and singing. He learned many of his songs from his father while in San Jon. He attributes his love for western swing music to the teachings of a black camp cook he knew while growing up, which helps explain the great soulfulness in his singing. Reed wrangled at Bob Crosby's ranch briefly and was the ranch foreman for the Mescalero Apache Indian tribe. In 1949, he was recorded by Folkways Records. Included in *Frontier and Cowboy Songs* are two cutting-horse tributes he wrote—"Miss Aleto" and "Powderhorn." Ray Reed heads the annual Lincoln County Cowboy Symposium in Ruidoso, New Mexico.

## DUANE DICKINSON

*Born in Scoby, Montana, February 19, 1931*

Duane Dickinson is a native Montana rancher/farmer who is considered an important collector of early cowboy songs and sentimental Victorian ballads. Duane is an occasional performer at gatherings in the West with a war bag of eclectic material that other cowboy singers love to learn.

Duane sometimes appears live with multi-instrumentalist Dick Dillof as the Double-D Drifters, performing traditional cowboy music, and with Bob and Fran Wilkins as Buck-brush, singing the western harmony song of the thirties and forties. He has self-released four cassettes of old-time cowboy songs under the titles of *Following the Long Trail With Duane Dickinson, Volumes I–IV*.

**Ray Reed. (Photograph courtesy of Ray Reed.)**

**Duane Dickinson. (*Song of the West* collection.)**

# Ramblin' Jack Elliott

**Hard Travelin': songs by Woody Guthrie and others**

Ramblin' Jack Elliott on the cover of *Hard Travelin': Songs by Woody Guthrie and Others*, 1989, Fantasy, Inc. (*Song of the West* collection.)

## "RAMBLIN'" JACK ELLIOTT (ELLIOTT CHARLES ADNOPOZ)

*Born in Brooklyn, New York, August 1, 1931*

A singular nomadic folk singer born in Brooklyn, Ramblin' Jack adapted the romance of the West and the cowboy way to his life. He left home at the age of fourteen when he saw a cowboy ride by. He followed the cowpoke and joined up with a fair, eventually hitchhiking west to a ranch. After trying his hand at cowboying and rodeoing, he returned to New York. In Greenwich Village he met Woody Guthrie, who was to be a profound influence on him.

In his live appearances, Jack is a mesmerizing performer whose personal charisma has been likened to that of Woody Guthrie's. In 1975, Ramblin' Jack Elliott-admirer Bob Dylan included him in his monumental Rolling Thunder Tour, which also included Arlo Guthrie, Joan Baez, and Sam Shepard.

Ramblin' Jack Elliott is a favorite performer wherever he shows up. These days he can be found popping up in his ramblin' motor home at the Elko Cowboy Poetry Gathering, where a crowd grows around him whenever he picks up his guitar. Although he has made thirty-three recordings on various labels, they do not reveal what a magnetic presence he is when performing.

## HARRY JACKSON

*Born in Chicago, Illinois, April 18, 1924*

Harry Jackson is one of the most authentic performers of cowboy song and lore. Without a guitar, backing band, or orchestra, Jackson ably performs scores of cowpoke whoops, hollers, and songs. He is well known as a master of cowboy art through his painting and sculpture.

Jackson learned his first cowboy songs from a retired cowboy who handled horses at the Chicago Stockyards. He left high school at the age of fourteen to cowboy in Wyoming, and he cowboyed at a number of ranches, including Earl Martin's Lazy A, the Pitchfork, the River, and the Whitt Ranch. He learned more cowboy songs while trying his hand at rodeoing. After a stint in the Marines during the Second World War, he moved to New York where he sculpted bronze and painted. He maintains an art studio in Cody, Wyoming.

Harry Jackson's major contribution to cowboy music is his two-record set *The Cowboy: His Songs, Ballads, and Brag Talk* (Folkways, 1959), a mammoth thirty-track collection of cowboy songs, whoops, and hollers, performed a capella. His recording "The Pot Wrassler" appeared on the cowboy/western anthology *Back In the Saddle Again* (New World Records, 1983) and the cuts "Morning Grub Holler," "Round-up Cook," "Little Joe the Wrangler's Sister Nell," "Some Cowboy Brag Talk," and "Strawberry Roan" are essential recordings on *Cowboy Songs on Folkways* (Smithsonian/Folkways Records, 1991).

# GLENN OHRLIN

*Born in Minneapolis, Minnesota,*
*October 26, 1926*

A cowboy folk singer and guitarist, Glen Ohrlin was raised just north of White Earth Indian Reservation in Winger, Minnesota. His illustrious past includes breaking colts at age twelve and buckarooing in Nevada, Wyoming, and Arizona, as well as rodeoing from 1943 through 1965. Since 1945, he has ranched in the Arkansas Ozarks.

In 1963, Ohrlin performed his first university concert in Illinois and credits Archie Green for getting him into the business. Glenn Ohrlin has played festivals and concerts ever since. His albums include *Hell-Bound Train* (Philo, 1964), *Cowboy Songs* (Philo, 1972), and *The Wild Buckaroo* (Rounder, 1984). Ohrlin's greatest contribution to cowboy music remains his scholarly cowboy songbook *The Hell-Bound Train* (University of Illinois, 1973).

FOLKWAYS RECORDS FH 5723

## HARRY JACKSON
## THE COWBOY HIS SONGS, BALLADS & BRAG TALK

Edited and Annotated by Kenneth S. Goldstein

**Harry Jackson on the cover of *Harry Jackson the Cowboy: His Songs, Ballads, and Brag Talk,* 1965, Folkways Records. (Courtesy Smithsonian/Folkways Recordings.)**

**Glenn Ohrlin. (*Song of the West* collection.)**

## BUCK RAMSEY

*Born in New Home, Texas, January 9, 1938*

**B**uck Ramsey is both a cowboy poet and singer. He grew up between the Texas panhandle towns of Dumas and Channing, in Middle Well. Although the son of farmers, he fell in love with the cowboying life from what he learned at the Coldwater Cattle Company, the Kilgore Ranch, and from his Uncle Ed.

A back injury in 1963 ended Ramsey's cowboying days, and he turned to writing poetry and singing cowboy songs. He is acknowledged as one of the finest traditional cowboy singers alive, and his album of classic cowboy songs *Rolling Uphill From Texas*, won the 1992 Western Heritage Award for traditional cowboy song. His book and corresponding album of poetry *And As I Rode Out on the Morning* contains his classic poem "Anthem." His most recent album is *My Home It Was In Texas*, 1994.

BUCK RAMSEY: ROLLING UPHILL FROM TEXAS

photography: Wyatt McSpadden

**(Photo by Wyatt McSpadden.)**

# THE GILLETTE BROTHERS

*Born Guy Gillette in Crockett, Texas, September 10, 1945, and Pipp Gillette in Staten Island, New York, February 16, 1950*

A highly enjoyable Texas duo, the Gillette Brothers are contemporary cowboy singers. The brothers were professional musicians for over fifteen years before taking over the family's Gillette Ranch, which was founded in 1912. Today the Gillette Ranch has its own cattle operation and is quite proud of its restored chuck wagons, which are entered at ranch cook-offs and contests.

The recent public re-interest in cowboy music and poetry has encouraged the brothers to combine their long love and interest of the West with their musical abilities. In 1992, they released *Home Ranch* on their own Big Daddy Records, and in 1994 released *Cinch Up Your Riggin'*.

**The Gillette Brothers, Pip (left) and Guy (right). (Photograph by Guy Gillette, Sr.)**

# WESTERN SWING

## WESTERN SWING MUSIC

*Guy Logsdon*

The term "western swing" may have been used occasionally before the early 1940s, but its widespread usage came from a promotional campaign for drawing crowds to Spade Cooley's dances on the Venice Pier (California) in the early forties.

This musical genre is difficult to define because it contains elements of many other musical forms such as pop, blues, jazz, Dixieland, traditional folk, fiddle, ragtime, and even an occasional touch of classical. Its origins are attempts to emulate big-band sounds on string instruments.

Western swing has been defined as a form of jazz, but jazz is equally hard to define. Rudi Blesh in *Shining Trumpets: A History of Jazz* (New York: Alfred A. Knopf, 1946) states that jazz is "spontaneous, improvised, though systematic, music, composed in the playing." Most western swing musicians were good at musical improvisation, but the Spade Cooley Orchestra, one of the all-time great western swing groups, always used arrangements, never improvising as an orchestra.

The word *swing*, when used as a musical form, is equally hard to define, but generally implies that a dance band improvises. The popular musical usage of the word grew in the mid-1930s and required a few years of growth before being applied to western dance music. The earlier descriptive terms for dance music used by recording companies on their labels were "hot" and "sweet." Hot dance music implied the use of some improvisations even in recording sessions, while sweet dance music indicated the adherence to arrangements. The labels on the recordings of western swing pioneers such as those of Bob Wills and the Texas Playboys often stated "hot dance band."

It is easier to describe western swing than to define it. It is ballroom-dance music with a western flair played primarily on string instruments. Yet, horns were and are used in many western swing bands. Swing is also characterized as having an emphasis on heavy rhythm sound, utilizing improvisation. In its early stages of development, it was music played primarily by Texas and Oklahoma musicians under the leadership of Bob Wills and Milton Brown and more accurately could be called southwestern music. However, since the musical sounds spread throughout the West, this musical genre truly became "western swing."

## WESTERN SWING SOCIETY

This nonprofit organization was founded in 1981 "to preserve and perpetuate the American art form known as Western Swing." They established the Western Swing Hall of Fame with induction ceremonies each October. The Society meets the first Sunday of each month at the Sacramento, California, Country Club Lanes Skyroom. The meeting always includes music and dancing. The Society address is P.O. Box 1775, North Highlands, California, 95660; membership includes their monthly newsletter *Western Swing Society Music News*.

## "TEX" SOLIE PAUL WILLIAMS

*Born in Ramsey, Illinois, August 23, 1917*

Tex Williams and the Western Caravan were a popular West Coast swing band from 1946 to 1957. Williams's deep voice was distinctive and had a quality few other singers could imitate. He grew up around music, because his father was an old-time fiddler. With family encouragement, he started his entertainment career early: at thirteen, he had his own radio show in Decatur, Illinois, using the name Jack Williams.

Williams worked in bands in the area until 1938, then he moved to Washington to pick apples. He soon became acquainted with musicians in the area and worked with a variety of small touring bands in the Northwest, where he met Spade Cooley. In 1942, he moved to Los Angeles and became an original member of Cooley's organization and, in 1943, was the vocalist on the hit recording "Shame, Shame On You."

In 1946, Williams left the Cooley organization to form his band, and a few excellent Cooley musicians went with him as the nucleus of the Western Caravan. The following year he recorded, "Smoke, Smoke, Smoke That Cigarette," cowritten with Merle Travis for Capitol. It became the number one country/western hit in 1947.

Williams enjoyed international success through his recordings, television and radio shows, and personal appearances. He recorded for RCA, Decca, Liberty, and smaller labels, but after the music entertainment world changed in the 1950s, his style of music became less popular. He did make it back into the charts in 1971 with "The Night Miss Nancy Ann's Hotel for Single Girls Burned Down." When he died on October 11, 1985, the music world lost one of its great baritone-bass singers and bandleaders.

**Tex Williams. (Guy Logsdon and the Ranch House Library.)**

# HENRY ALFRED "AL" CLAUSER AND HIS OKLAHOMA OUTLAWS

*Born in Manitoba, Illinois, in 1911*

Al Clauser started his musical career while in high school, organizing a trio and playing clubs in the Peoria, Illinois, area. The trio was soon given airtime over Peoria station WMBD and grew to a five-member band. He hired musicians who played two or more instruments, creating a sound larger than its six members, and took pride in the jazz sound of his predominantly string band. In later years, he recalled, "We always played diminished and augmented chords."

With equal pride, he also claimed to be the first to use the term "western swing" as early as 1928. He chose the name "Oklahoma Outlaws" because the brand of string swing music played needed a western tone and a name "that would stick," even though none of the band members had ever been to Oklahoma.

In 1934, the Outlaws moved their show and base of operation to WHO, Des Moines, Iowa, then in 1938 they moved to WCKY, the CBS affiliate in Cincinnati, Ohio. After one year, they changed to KHBF, Rock Island, Illinois, where their show was carried over 272 Mutual Network stations. While still broadcasting at WHO in 1937, Al's friend Gene Autry called Al and the band to work in the movie *Rootin' Tootin' Rhythm*, and while in Los Angeles, they recorded twelve sides for ARC Records.

During World War II, the band moved to Tulsa, Oklahoma, to work in airplane defense plants. By the end of the war, the band had grown to nine members, competing with Johnnie Lee Wills and Leon McAuliffe for dance crowds. They broadcast daily over station KTUL and introduced twelve-year-old Clara Ann Fowler, who became known professionally as Patti Page. She made her first recording with Al Clauser and his Oklahoma Outlaws.

In the 1950s, when television and rock music slowly killed large dance bands, Al and the Outlaws disbanded. Al continued his career in broadcasting by working for KTUL Television in Tulsa; he is fondly remembered as "Uncle Zeke" for his work on a children's show. He remained in Tulsa until he died, March 3, 1989.

# TOMMY DOUGLAS ALLSUP

*Born in Owasso, Oklahoma, November 24, 1931*

Tommy Allsup not only is a major producer of country/western music, but also a premier western swing guitarist. As a session guitarist and record producer, he played a major role in putting swing into country music. He also leads one of the major Texas Playboy groups, for he grew up in Bob and Johnnie Lee Wills' country and worked for and with them.

Allsup became a member of the Johnnie Lee Wills band in 1952 and later became a member of Buddy Holly's Crickets. It was his background in Tulsa swing that gave new depth to Holly's beat. Allsup flipped a coin with Richie Valens that night in Iowa and lost. He rode the bus, and Holly, Valens, and others were killed in the airplane crash. Allsup continued his life in country/western music as a tribute to the Wills/Holly legacies and his own musical skills.

**Al Clauser and His Oklahoma Outlaws, 1937. (Guy Logsdon and the Ranch House Library.)**

In the 1960s, Allsup produced records for Liberty that included Willie Nelson's 1960s records, the Bob Wills records on Liberty, Asleep At the Wheel's first five records, Tex Williams, Mickey Gilley, Gene Watson, and others. It was Allsup who produced *For the Last Time*, the legendary western-swing tribute to Bob Wills. In addition, he has been the session guitarist for over 6500 recordings and has arranged background music for many cowboy poets. He works as an independent music producer in Nashville and has produced two cassettes featuring his guitar style: *Tommy Allsup: 10 Great Country Classics* and *Tommy Allsup: 10 Great Gospel Classics.*

# BOBBY BOATRIGHT

*Born in Denison, Texas, September 30, 1939*

A great and popular swing fiddler, Boatright was born into a musical family. He started his fiddling career at the age of eleven, playing in a band of youngsters, appearing on shows such as the "Big D Jamboree" in Dallas, and at the age of fourteen he became a member of a teenage band led by Bill Mack. While developing his musical skills, he also maintained his grades and interest in education, eventually earning masters degrees in math and physics.

Boatright spent many years as a faculty member at Weatherford (Texas) Junior College, teaching math and physics as well as working in numerous western swing bands. He was a member of the Original Texas Playboys and continues to work with Texas Playboy groups as well as with other western swing bands. He lives in Mansfield, Texas, and was inducted into the Western Swing Hall of Fame in 1988.

# YODELING POLKA

By SPADE COOLEY, LARRY (Pedro) DE PAUL and ANDREW SOLDI

*Recorded for Columbia Records by* **SPADE COOLEY**

Spade Cooley on the cover of "Yodeling Polka," 1947. (Guy Logsdon and the Ranch House Library.)

# DONNELL CLYDE "SPADE" COOLEY

*Born in Grande, Oklahoma, December 17, 1910*

Cooley, who was one-quarter Cherokee, studied violin and cello at Chemawa Indian School in Oregon and was groomed for the concert stage, but concert music was not his interest. The hard times of the 1930s took his family to Modesto, California, trying to find a better life, and he did earn some money as a violinist.

In 1941, he organized his own band, using members of Rudy Sooter's band for the nucleus. They played the Venice Pier Ballroom for eighteen months, and it was there that Cooley was given the appellation "King of Western Swing."

Cooley leased the Riverside Rancho in 1943, enjoying growing popularity because his arrangements and musical style appealed to West Coast dancers. In 1946, he leased the Santa Monica Ballroom, which became the first televised ballroom dancing show. He won two Emmy awards for the show. His sound emphasized fiddles voiced above the lead line while using other instruments often heard in orchestras, such as a harp, and his "western orchestra" strictly followed arrangements. They played everything from traditional hoedowns to boogie woogie—whatever was popular. However, when he toured Oklahoma and Texas, his brand of music was not accepted in the Bob and Johnnie Lee Wills country, and he had to borrow money to get the orchestra back to California.

Musical shorts were filmed for movie theaters, and Cooley and the band appeared in motion pictures. He enjoyed radio and television popularity in the 1950s, but as with most large western dance bands in that decade, his popularity was eroded by television and the changing entertainment tastes of the public. Then in 1961, he murdered his wife, and received a penitentiary sentence. In November 1969, he was released to make an appearance at a sheriff's benefit show in Oakland, California, where he died from a heart attack.

Alvin Crow. (Guy Logsdon and the Ranch House Library.)

## ALVIN CROW AND THE PLEASANT VALLEY BOYS

*Birth information not found*

Crow, one of the Austin, Texas, musicians who gained fame and popularity in the "redneck and outlaw" music era of the 1970s, had a style of music best described as rocking Oklahoma swing. He is a native of Oklahoma and grew up hearing western swing sounds, adapting his fiddle and band style to contemporary dance interests while maintaining a strong Bob Wills influence. His first regional hit was "Nyquil Blues," and even though he has not become a superstar, he has continued to play the music he loves and to enjoy Southwestern popularity.

## THERON EUGENE "TED" DAFFAN

*Born in Beauregarde Parish, Louisiana, September 21, 1912*

Ted Daffan wrote the first truck driver song, "Truck Drivers' Blues," in 1938 and later wrote the classic "Born to Lose." He grew up in the Houston, Texas, area and taught himself to play Hawaiian-style guitar before changing to the steel guitar. In 1933, he had his own Hawaiian-style band, "The Blue Islanders," in Houston, and the following year he joined the Blue Ridge Playboys as a steel player. Later, he joined the Bar X Cowboys, again as a steel player, staying with them until he organized his own band, The Texans, in 1940.

Fronting his own band, Daffan had his first recording session for Columbia Records on April 25, 1940, in Dallas, eventually recording twenty-four sides. In that first session he recorded "Worried Mind," his first hit song. On February 20, 1942, in Hollywood, he recorded "Born to Lose" and "No Letter Today," along with other sides, but those two songs were released on the same disc and earned Daffan a Gold Record. He used the pseudonym "Frankie Brown" for the songwriter credits.

World War II broke up his band, and in 1944, he was hired to front a band at the Venice Pier Ballroom in California. He returned to Texas in 1946 and later moved to Nashville for a stint at writing and publishing songs before returning to Houston. Ted Daffan wrote many popular songs and a few major hits.

Ted Daffan on the cover of *Ted Daffan's Coin Machine Hits,* published by Peer International Corporation, 1944. (Guy Logsdon and the Ranch House Library.)

**Tommy Duncan and the Western All-Stars, 1949. (Guy Logsdon and the Ranch House Library.)**

# TOMMY DUNCAN

*Born in Hillsboro, Texas, January 11, 1911*

Tommy Duncan is best remembered as the popular vocalist with Bob Wills and the Texas Playboys. He started his singing career at the age of twelve, impersonating a female singer, and in 1930 with his first radio appearance behind him in Amarillo, he joined a dance band in Fort Worth. When Milton Brown left the Lightcrust Doughboys, Duncan auditioned and replaced Brown. At that time, his singing style was an imitation of Jimmie Rodgers.

When Bob Wills left the Doughboy program in 1933, Duncan went with him to Waco, Texas, and to Tulsa, Oklahoma. As the Playboys slowly changed their style of music, Duncan developed his own vocal style of phrasing lyrics and became a major influence on decades of singers who followed. However, while he and Wills appeared to be friends on the stage, offstage they weren't, and in 1948, Wills fired Duncan. A few members of the Playboys followed him, forming a short-lived group called Tommy Duncan and the Western All-Stars.

When this band dissolved, Duncan traveled as a singer performing with local or pickup bands until he and Wills joined forces again in the early 1960s, recording for Liberty Records. Even though they were not friends, Duncan and Wills were considered to be a team and neither did well after the split. For a short time with Liberty, they regained the spirit that made them popular. Yet, within a year, their differences separated them once again. Tommy Duncan died from a heart attack on July 25, 1967.

**Merl Lindsay and His Oklahoma Night-Riders. (Guy Logsdon and the Ranch House Library.)**

# MERL LINDSAY AND HIS OKLAHOMA NIGHT RIDERS
## (MERLE LINDSAY SALATHIEL)

*Born in Oklahoma in 1915*

Merl Lindsay and His Oklahoma Night Riders was a major western swing band in the forties and fifties. He was one of eight children born into a musical family, for both parents were musicians and a brother and sister became professional musicians. He started his career in 1936 in a family-owned dance hall, Salathiel's Barn, in Oklahoma City. Two years later, he formed his own band, Merle Salathiel and the Barnyard Boys, and in 1941, moved them to California with the name Oklahoma Night Riders. While there, they appeared in a few movies, and he dropped his last name and changed the spelling of Merle to Merl.

In 1947, Lindsay returned to Oklahoma City where he broadcast a daily noonday radio show and a television show. That year the family dance hall burned, so he and the Night Riders worked a variety of dance halls until he opened the Lindsay Land Ballroom in south Oklahoma City. They recorded for Mercury Records, MGM Records, and other labels, enjoying regional popularity.

In 1957, Red Foley featured them on his "Ozark Jubilee" television show and hired them as the regular show band. They changed their name to the Ozark Jubilee Band. Many of the band members moved back and forth from his band to other western swing bands, such as those led by Bob Wills, Johnnie Lee Wills, Leon McAuliffe, and Hank Thompson.

Merle Lindsay Salathiel died from cancer on October 12, 1965, in Oklahoma City and was posthumously inducted into the Western Swing Hall of Fame in 1992.

# EAST TEXAS SERENADERS

*Birth information not found*

The recordings made by this string band are representative of western house-party music that developed into western swing-ballroom-dance music. The leader of this small band from Lindale and Mineola, Texas, was Daniel Huggins Williams, fiddle; the other members were Cloet Hamman, guitar; John Munnerlyn, tenor banjo; and Henry Bogan, cello. They started working together as young men with no intention of becoming professional musicians, but their danceable rhythm made them a "sought after" group. They played the popular dance tunes of the time, not just breakdown tunes; in fact, square dancing was not very popular—it was round dancing that people enjoyed. They recorded for Columbia on December 2, 1927, and later cut sides for Brunswick and Decca. By the mid-1930s, the call of other occupations broke up this western string dance band.

# CURLY LEWIS

*Born near Stigler, Oklahoma, in 1924*

One of the all-time great western swing fiddlers and vocalists, Lewis was the fifth of nine children of Cherokee Indian descent. His father taught all of the children to play an instrument, and eventually Curly learned nine different instruments. At the age of eleven, he won a Bob Wills fiddling contest in Tulsa against sixty-seven older men.

In 1945, Lewis joined the Johnnie Lee Wills Band as a guitarist, and later moved to the front-line fiddling position. Later, he became a Texas Playboy with Bob Wills, worked in Leon McAuliffe's Cimmaron Band, and spent eleven years with Hank Thompson and the Brazos Valley Boys. He lives in Tulsa, Oklahoma, and appears with Texas Playboy bands. In 1990, Curly Lewis was inducted into the Western Swing Hall of Fame.

**O. W. Mayo. (Guy Logsdon and the Ranch House Library.)**

# O. W. MAYO

*Born in northeastern Mississippi, January 17, 1901*

O. W. Mayo was the business manager for Bob Wills and the Texas Playboys, for Johnnie Lee Wills and All His Boys, and was owner of the legendary Cain's Ballroom for over thirty years. The Wills family and those who know him well so respected him that they always referred to him and still call him Mr. Mayo.

Mr. Mayo left Mississippi at the age of eighteen and moved to Waco, Texas, where he worked for a railroad. Later he worked for a petroleum company and had the opportunity to advance to a better position in the firm when he met Bob Wills in the fall of 1933. He promoted a Wills dance and slowly became involved in promoting other dances. Deciding to stay with Bob and the band as their business manager/promoter, he was a factor in their decision to move to Oklahoma. It was Bob and he who traveled to Tulsa on February 9, 1934, and obtained a trial broadcast over KVOO Radio.

Mr. Mayo wrote "Blues for Dixie" and other songs, worked as a Wills radio and dance announcer, wrote poetry, and managed the Bob Wills and Johnnie Lee Wills rodeos for over forty years. His rodeo knowledge and activities earned committee assignments in the Rodeo Cowboys Association and recognition as a major contributor to the growth and popularity of the rodeo sport. In the music world, he played a major role in the development of western swing. O. W. Mayo still resides in Tulsa.

**The Original Texas Playboys. (Guy Logsdon and the Ranch House Library.)**

## THE ORIGINAL TEXAS PLAYBOYS

*Birth information not found*

After the death of Bob Wills in 1975, Leon McAuliffe and Bob's widow, Betty Wills, collaborated to perpetuate the memory of Bob. McAuliffe organized a few Playboy veterans with younger musicians who grew up playing the Wills sound and occasionally working with Bob in pickup bands. The original group included Jack Stidham, fiddle; Bob Boatright, fiddle; Joe Ferguson, bass; Leon Rausch, vocalist; Al Strickland, piano; Smokey Dacus, drums; Bob Kiser, guitar; Rudy Martin, clarinet; and Leon McAuliffe, steel guitar.

Gene Gasaway replaced Stidham as a fiddler, and in the following ten years other members changed, with the most significant addition being Eldon Shamblin, guitar. When Al Strickland died, he was replaced with the Johnnie Lee Wills piano man Clarence Cagle. After McAuliffe died in 1989, the group continued under the leadership of Leon Rausch but disbanded during the early 1990s. Other groups continue to bill themselves as Texas Playboys, but they are all "former" Playboys, not the original.

## HOYLE NIX

*Born in Azel, Texas, March 22, 1918*

Hoyle Nix and His West Texas Cowboys played the western swing sounds of the Wills family for nearly forty years in the Big Springs, Texas, area. In 1954, he opened his dance hall, the Stampede, in Big Springs and played dances four nights a week. He also contributed to the popularity of western swing by writing "Big Balls in Cowtown." Fans believe that Nix and his dance hall were the last source for hard-core Wills-style western swing dancing. He died August 21, 1985, but his son, Jody, carries on the Nix/Wills/Big Springs traditions.

## JOHNNIE LEE WILLS

*Born in Hall County, Texas, September 2, 1912*

Johnnie Lee was the second of four sons born to John and Emma Wills, who were tenant cotton farmers in Texas. His brother Bob Wills, one of the original Light Crust Doughboys, wrangled a job at the mill for Johnnie Lee. When Bob left the mill and the Doughboys in September 1933 to form his own band in Waco, Texas, he took Johnnie Lee with him and said that he had to play the tenor banjo, which was a rhythm instrument used by many dance bands. Bob and the band moved to Tulsa in 1934; Johnnie Lee was one of the original Texas Playboys.

As the band grew, changed sounds, and had more bookings than they could play, Bob made Johnnie Lee front his own band; however, Johnnie Lee was a shy, quiet man who was reluctant to lead a band. In 1938, his first band was called the Rhythmaires and did not gain a wide following; so, in 1940, he and his father moved a band to Fort Smith, Arkansas, where, once again, popularity failed. Johnnie Lee then reorganized in Tulsa with a few musicians from the Alabama Boys and slowly developed his own fans.

In the summer of 1942, Bob decided to move to Hollywood and made Johnnie Lee take the KVOO broadcasts, the Thursday and Saturday night dances at Cain's Ballroom, and the annual rodeo. Again, with reluctance, Johnnie Lee did it and developed a band that at times was bigger and better than the Texas Playboys, often with as many as thirteen members, many of whom doubled on instruments. He also developed a loyal following,

because he was truly a friend to all fans, and he became a great band leader. Many western swing fans say that they grew up hearing Bob Wills over KVOO, when they actually listened to Johnnie Lee Wills and All His Boys.

When he fronted his band, Johnnie Lee played the fiddle, and it was he, not Bob, who made "Milk Cow Blues" popular in the 1940s, recorded for Decca Records. He was the first to record "Peter Cottontail" on the Bullet label, and his recording of "Rag Mop" played a major role in changing the sounds of country/western music. When he left KVOO in 1958, Johnnie Lee had the longest continuous daytime radio program in the nation, and he worked as many years as his brother in leading a large western swing band.

In the summer of 1982, Johnnie Lee Wills and All His Boys represented the State of Oklahoma at the Smithsonian Institution Annual Festival of American Folklife in Washington, D.C., and attracted some of the largest crowds in festival history. Johnnie Lee Wills died in Tulsa, October 25, 1984.

## HERBERT CLAYTON "HANK" PENNY

*Born in Birmingham, Alabama, September 17, 1918*

Hank Penny was one of many talented musicians born east of the Mississippi who became identified with music west of the great river. Best known as the composer of "Won't You Ride My Little Red Wagon," Penny worked his way out of coal mining with musical and comedic skills. His early success was over both WWL in New Orleans and WLW in Cincinnati, and in 1944 he landed in Los Angeles. He soon became associated with Merle Travis, Spade Cooley, and other leading California musicians and became a moderately successful western swing bandleader and recording artist. Comedy became his trademark, even though he was a talented musician/songwriter. Penny died of a heart attack, April 17, 1992.

**Johnnie Lee Wills and All His Boys, Cain's Ballroom, Tulsa, Oklahoma, 1951. (Guy Logsdon and the Ranch House Library.)**

The Alabama Boys in
Tulsa, Oklahoma, 1938.
(Guy Logsdon and the
Ranch House Library.)

Photo caption text within image:
The Original ALABAMA BOYS
1938
Southwest's Greatest String Band!
—ON THE AIR—
KTUL DAILY 1:00 P.M.
TULSA

"HELLO TO ALL OUR FRIENDS"
Left to Right
Carl Rainwater    Roy Johnson
Dave Edwards      Otis Thompson
Jerry Byler       Ebb Gray
Harley Huggins    Jack McElroy
Cotton Thompson   Charles Adams

# THE ALABAMA BOYS

*Birth information not found*

Don Ivey was an early member of the Texas Playboys in Tulsa, but his not showing up for rehearsals, combined with other problems, forced Bob Wills to fire him. It was 1935, and Ivey decided to organize a band to compete with Wills. He went to Texas and got Guy "Cotton" Thompson and in Shawnee, Oklahoma, hired Louis and Mancel Tierney and Harley Huggins. With other musicians they started broadcasting over KVOO, but Ivey could not get along with the band members. He left the band and Allen Franklin became the manager. The band members brought in other Oklahomans such as Eldon Shamblin, guitar; Ray DeGeer, saxophone; and Charles Laughton, trumpet. They were successfully competing with Wills, because they had the Playmore Ballroom as their home dance base.

Franklin left the group, and David T. Edwards, who was a grocer, took over their promotion and management, but he was not experienced in dance promotion. Many of the members left and became Texas Playboys. They brought new members in from the Tulsa area such as guitarist Junior Bernard. They broadcasted over KTUL and recorded a few sides for Decca Records, but could not regain their musical strength. When Johnnie Lee Wills organized his band in 1940, most of the members came from the Alabama Boys. With World War II pulling many musicians away, the Alabama Boys disbanded by 1942, but their place in musical history lies in their bringing the many talented and legendary musicians to the Bob and Johnnie Lee Wills' organizations.

# JAMES "JIM" BOYD

*Born September 28, 1914, in Fannin County, Texas*

A younger brother of Bill Boyd, Jim was the original bass player for the Cowboy Ramblers, assuming the leadership role when Bill was away. He worked in the Light Crust Doughboy organization in 1938 and 1939, and later had his own band, The Men of the West, who recorded for RCA between 1949 and 1951. Jim Boyd died March 11, 1993.

# MILTON BROWN

*Born in Stephenville, Texas, September 8, 1903*

Milton Brown is considered to be a cofounder of western swing; some fans believe that he was "the" founder. It was 1931 when Brown, a cigar salesman, heard Bob Wills and Herman Arnspiger playing at a Fort Worth house dance and asked to sing a few songs with them; they liked his voice and included him in subsequent engagements. Working as a trio under different names, they talked W. Lee O'Daniel, general manager of Forth Worth's Burrus Mills, into sponsoring them. They became the Light Crust Doughboys.

Brown enjoyed playing dances, but O'Daniel insisted on radio, stage, and nondancing appearances. Brown left the Doughboys in September 1932 and organized his own dance band, Milton Brown and His Musical Brownies. He was a vocalist and played no musical instrument in the band; he hired his brother, Durwood Brown, guitar; Jesse Ashlock, fiddle; Wanna Coffman, bass; and Ocie Stockard, tenor banjo. Within a few weeks, he added Cecil Brower, fiddle, and Fred Calhoun, piano. They broadcast over KTAT, Fort Worth, and played regularly at the Crystal Springs Dance Pavilion. In a short time, the Brownies were a popular dance band.

On April 4, 1934, in the Texas Hotel, San Antonio, the Brownies recorded eight sides for Victor Records and recorded ten more songs for Victor a month later. Their popularity continued to grow, and Decca Records signed them away from Victor. They traveled to Chicago and recorded thir-

ty-six songs on January 27–28, 1935, and by then Brown had hired Bob Dunn, the first man known to amplify a steel guitar. Cliff Bruner, another great fiddler, joined them before their next sessions in 1936.

The sounds they played made them one of the hot dance bands with great potential, but Milton Brown was in a car wreck while returning home from a Crystal Springs dance. The young nursing student with him was killed, and in the hospital his condition worsened with complications of pneumonia. Brown died April 18, 1936. His brother led the band for approximately one year before disbanding it.

Milton Brown and Bob Wills were good friends, and it will never be known if Brown and the Musical Brownies would have gained the fame and recognition that Bob Wills received. Brown rarely used horns in the band, but had he lived, he may have added them. His rhythm was not as heavy as Wills's, and according to their original partner, Herman Arnspiger, Milton Brown did not have the charisma that Bob Wills had.

**Milton Brown on the cover of *Country and Western Dance-O-Rama: Milton Brown and His Brownies*, Western Records. (Guy Logsdon and the Ranch House Library.)**

## WILLIAM LEON McAULIFFE

*Born in Houston, Texas, January 3, 1917*

On the 1936 recording of "Steel Guitar Rag" when Bob Wills said, "Take it away, Leon," he started a saying that is still heard and created a star, Leon McAuliffe. Late in life, McAuliffe credited Wills with making him famous, though it is possible that he may have become a popular musician without Wills, because he had the ambition and drive to become a major western swing bandleader as well as a steel guitar pioneer.

He started his career as a teenager, joining the Light Crust Doughboys in Fort Worth, and in 1935, at the age of eighteen, Bob Wills hired him as a member of the Texas Playboys in Tulsa. As a member of the Playboys, he probably had more influence in making the steel guitar popular and a front-line band instrument in the 1930s than did any other steel guitar player. He and Eldon Shamblin were the first to record steel guitar and standard guitar duets.

McAuliffe left the Playboys for the navy during World War II and, following his discharge, organized his own western swing band in Tulsa, where Tulsa's Cimarron Ballroom became headquarters for his weekly dances and radio and television shows. Competing with Johnnie Lee Wills and Cain's Ballroom for dance popularity, he earned a loyal following. Later, he became a licensed pilot and the owner of radio station KAMO in Rogers, Arkansas, before disbanding in 1968.

McAuliffe organized and led the Original Texas Playboys in the 1970s and 1980s; he died in Tulsa, August 20, 1988.

## TOM MORRELL

*Born in Dallas, Texas, October 31, 1938*

Tom Morrell has made appearances at many cowboy gatherings in the 1990s and has been the steel guitar player on numerous cowboy song and western swing recordings that come out of Texas. He coproduced two award-winning Don Edward's albums, *Cowtown Blues & Desert Nights* and *Chant of the Wanderer*. He designs steel guitars and has worked with western swing legends, such as the Texas Playboys, Tex Williams, Hank Penny, Ray Price, Red Steagall, and many more. Morrell lives in Little Elm, Texas, and appears regularly with the Time-Warp Tophands.

## CLIFF BRUNER

*Born in Texas City, Texas, April 25, 1915*

At the age of four, Cliff Bruner learned to play the fiddle; ten years later he was wandering around Texas as a young musician. He became a jazz and swing fiddler in contrast to breakdown fiddlers, working in many different bands, playing fiddle and mandolin. It is probable that he was the first to amplify a mandolin, and he was a member of the Musical Brownies when Milton Brown died. Many members of that band joined Bruner in forming the Texas Wanderers, but he brought in additional men who are legendary western swing figures. They recorded for Decca Records and broadcast over KXYZ, Houston, remaining organized as a popular dance band until the mid-1940s. Cliff Bruner continued to work as a legendary western swing musician, making an appearance as late as 1992 at the Cowboy Symposium in Glencoe, New Mexico.

**Leon McAuliffe. (Guy Logsdon and the Ranch House Library.)**

# W. LEE O'DANIEL
## (WILBERT LEE O'DANIEL)

*Born in Malta, Ohio, March 11, 1890*

**W**. Lee O'Daniel was a politician who learned that he could gain office through country/hillbilly music. He grew up in Kansas and went to Texas as a flour salesman, rising to general manager with Burrus Mills in Fort Worth. He did not like the music Bob Wills, Milton Brown, and Herman Arnspiger played, but their popularity demanded that Burrus Mills sponsor them. Enjoying their success, O'Daniel fronted the Light Crust Doughboys as the announcer and contributed poetry and songs such as "Beautiful Texas" to the programs.

In 1935, O'Daniel left Burrus Mills and formed Hillbilly Flour, organizing his band, the Hillbilly Boys, and letting Leon Huff, who later became Johnnie Lee Wills's vocalist, lead the band. Using the Hillbilly Boys at his political rallies and giving speeches over border radio stations, O'Daniel was elected governor and later United States senator from Texas.

**Tom Morrell. (Photograph courtesty of Tom Morrell.)**

**W. Lee O'Daniel on the cover of "Beautiful Texas" (Shapiro, Bernstein, and Company). (Guy Logsdon and the Ranch House Library.)**

**Jimmie Revard and His Oklahoma Playboys on the cover of *Oh! Swing It*, Mutual Music Corporation, 1982. (Guy Logsdon and the Ranch House Library.)**

# JIMMIE REVARD AND HIS SWING OKLAHOMA PLAYBOYS

*Birth information not found*

Jimmie Revard and His Swing Oklahoma Playboys were based in San Antonio, Texas, between 1936 and 1938. Revard was born in Pawhuska, Oklahoma, and was one-fourth Osage Indian. The family moved to the San Antonio area when he was a youngster, where he studied violin. In 1936, he decided to put together a radio/dance band, and, no doubt, the growing popularity of Bob Wills and the Texas Playboys based in Oklahoma inspired the band to name themselves the Oklahoma Playboys from San Antonio. In a short time, they became an eight-piece band and started broadcasting over KMAC, eventually being featured over WOAI, a 50,000-watt station. They recorded for Victor Records and enjoyed regional popularity before moving to Pittsburgh, Kansas. By 1939, Revard lost his desire to be a bandleader, and the vocalist/guitar player, Adolph Hofner, took the band back to Texas.

# OLE RASMUSSEN AND HIS CORNHUSKERS

*Birth information not found*

When Bob Wills was the most popular western swing band in the nation and possibly the highest-paid dance band, imitators could be found throughout the West. Ole Rasmussen from Nebraska became a master Wills imitator. He organized a dance band on the West Coast and traveled up and down, imitating the Wills's sound. They recorded for Capitol Records using some original songs played in the Wills's style. It was the only band that angered Bob Wills when he heard them.

# "HANK" HENRY WILLIAM THOMPSON

*Born in Waco, Texas, September 3, 1925*

Hank Thompson has been a giant in western swing for over forty-five years and has helped transform swing music into an industry. He learned to play on a four-dollar guitar that his parents gave him, and as a teenager, he earned his own radio show on WACO as "Hank, the Hired Hand," sponsored by a local flour company. Seven days after graduating from high school in 1943, he signed up for service in the navy—a thirty-seven-month tour.

When discharged, Thompson returned to Waco and his own radio show on KWTX, and he organized his western swing band, naming them The Brazos Valley Boys. In August 1946 he recorded "Whoa Sailor!" and "Swing Wide Your Gates of Love" (Globe 124) for Globe Records in Los Angeles. They became regional hits, and when Tex Ritter heard them, he recommended that Capitol Records sign Thompson.

In 1948, Thompson and Capitol started a relationship that lasted eighteen years, with hits such as "Humpty Dumpty Heart," "Green Light," "Wild Side of Life" (a million seller in 1952), "Oklahoma Hills," and "Whoa, Sailor!" Hank Thompson became a nationally popular western swing star.

In 1952, Thompson decided to make his band the best in western swing, and since Bob Wills had moved to Texas, Hank chose to make Oklahoma City his base of operation. A few years later, he moved to Tulsa and worked there for over thirty

years. He hired quality musicians who helped him create a distinctive Thompson sound, and Jim Halsey became his manager and agent. Halsey booked him in northern and northeastern dance halls, and Hank Thompson became the first western swing artist to tour outside of the western states. Eventually, he became the first to take live western swing into foreign countries.

In the 1950s, Thompson and his band received numerous awards and for thirteen years were voted the best band by the disc jockeys. He was the first country/western artist to record in high fidelity and the first to record in stereo. In 1960, he became the first to record a live album, *Live at the Golden Nugget.* He followed this with live albums at the Cheyenne Rodeo and at the Texas State Fair.

In 1966, he changed to Warner Records and two years later went to Dot. Throughout the sixties and seventies, he continued to produce hit western swing recordings. In the late sixties, it became economically necessary to reduce the size of his band, and in the eighties, he returned to Texas and used local and pickup bands for his appearances. Hank Thompson now lives near Dallas and continues to make personal appearances.

## WESLEY WEBB "SPEEDY" WEST

*Born near Springfield, Missouri, January 25, 1924*

S peedy West had more to do with making the pedal steel guitar popular than any other musician. As a young boy he learned to play on a steel-bodied "National" guitar, using a knife handle for his bar. At the age of twenty-two and with a young family, West left the farm to try his hand at music in Southern California. He worked in a dry cleaning plant during the day and at night sat in with small bands at taverns and honky-tonks, developing his own musical style.

In 1947, West joined the Spade Cooley Orchestra and stayed with them for six months, working then with smaller swing bands. By 1948, he purchased the second pedal steel guitar manufactured by Paul Bigsby, who was the only one making pedal steels. West worked at creating a style using the volume control for effects and the pedals for musical slurs. He joined the Cliffe Stone organization, who broadcast the "Dinner Bell Roundup" radio show. This show became the popular Saturday night television/radio/dance show

**Bob Wills and His Texas Playboys at the Blue Moon Dance Pavilion in Tulsa, Oklahoma, 1939. This is the first time they wore western clothes. (Guy Logsdon and the Ranch House Library.)**

"Hometown Jamboree," in the El Monte Legion Stadium.

He and guitarist Jimmy Bryant recorded sixty-five singles and five albums for Capitol, and West became "the" session steel guitarist on the West Coast. Within a five-year period, he played for more than six-thousand recordings and 177 singers, including Dinah Shore, Frank Sinatra, Bing Crosby, Gene Autry, and Tex Ritter. When Tennessee Ernie Ford and Kay Starr recorded "I'll Never Be Free," he used his volume-control knob to make a special sound, and this hit record brought attention to the pedal steel guitar as the instrument to use instead of the nonpedal steel. In addition to using it for music, West recorded special sound effects for the Disney Studio. He is now retired and living in Broken Arrow, Oklahoma.

## JAMES ROBERT (JIM ROB) "BOB" WILLS

*Born in Limestone County, Texas, March 6, 1905*

**B**orn into a family of fiddlers, Bob Wills was destined to become the "Daddy of Western Swing." He started playing the fiddle as a youngster and was forced to use all of the bow, not just the upper end as breakdown fiddlers do, thus, developing a long-bow technique. The family moved to west Texas in 1913, and Wills started playing house dances with his father, John Wills.

In 1929, after working at a variety of jobs, including barbering and preaching, Wills moved to Fort Worth and worked in a blackface minstrel show, where he was approached by a young guitarist, Herman Arnspiger, to let him become a musical partner. While playing house dances in Fort Worth, Milton Brown, a cigar salesman/singer, started working with them. They became the original Light Crust Doughboys, broadcasting over KFJZ for Burrus Mills. When Brown left in 1932, he was replaced with Tommy Duncan.

In September 1933, Wills left the Doughboys and moved to Waco with his own band. He took Duncan, his brother Johnnie Lee Wills, and Kermit and June Whalin, two brothers working at the station. While broadcasting over WACO, the station manager and trumpet player Everett Stover started sitting in with them, and O. W. Mayo became their manager. In January 1934, they decided their future was in Oklahoma and moved to Oklahoma City and WKY radio. However, W. Lee O'Daniel, who fronted the Light Crust Doughboys and was the Burrus Mills manager, hated Wills and promised to buy airtime on WKY if they would cancel the Wills show. They did.

Wills and Mayo decided to try Tulsa and KVOO, which was a 25,000-watt station. At midnight, February 9, 1934, they played a one-hour trial broadcast and were so well received that they were given daily show time—KVOO and Tulsa became the voice of western swing. The original Texas Playboys were Bob Wills, Johnnie Lee Wills, Tommy Duncan, June and Kermit Whalin, Everett Stover, and O. W. Mayo, with Wills's cousin Son Lansford joining them.

The band grew more by accident than by plan, and the demand for dance dates grew daily. In 1935, they made Cain's Ballroom their headquarters and broadcast their noon show, Monday

**Billy Jack Wills.
(Photograph courtesy of
Lorene Wills.)**

through Saturday and their Thursday and Saturday night dances from there. By 1940, the Playboy organization had grown to a size comparable to any big swing band in the nation, and they could play over three thousand songs, whatever each dance crowd wanted to hear. Bob Wills and His Texas Playboys became the greatest western swing band ever assembled.

In 1940, the movie bug hit Wills when he and a few band members made a movie with Tex Ritter, *Take Me Back to Oklahoma.* In July 1942, he turned all Tulsa activities to Johnnie Lee Wills and made California his headquarters. However, World War II broke apart the Playboys organization, and when he reorganized in California, he primarily used string instruments. Then in 1948, he fired Tommy Duncan. Neither enjoyed the success they had when working as a team. As the big band era slowly faded, the size of Wills's band was reduced. He moved to Sacramento, then to Oklahoma City, and finally to Dallas but never regained the musical power he enjoyed in Tulsa.

In 1958, Wills took his brother's band in Tulsa and toured the Southwest. In 1960, he and Duncan joined forces again for recordings and a few personal appearances. This reunion did not last long, and Wills returned to using local bands for his appearances. There are probably 10,000 musicians in Texas who claim to have worked with Bob Wills and possibly did. Wills died May 13, 1975, and was buried in Tulsa alongside his parents, brothers, and sisters.

# BILLY JACK WILLS

*Born near Memphis, Texas, February 26, 1926*

As the youngest of the Wills brothers, he was referred to by Bob as "Baby Brother" and became a drummer and bass player. He joined the Playboys in California and moved back to Oklahoma with them in 1949. In the late forties, Billy Jack started writing songs and, by 1950 in Oklahoma City, finished the lyrics to an old family tune named "Faded Love." He cowrote "Lily Dale" with Tiny Moore, and other early rockabilly (possibly swingabilly) songs.

In 1950, Bob still owned Wills Point dance hall in Sacramento, and Tiny Moore talked him into reopening, then let him manage it. Bob sent Billy Jack to Wills Point to organize and direct the band, so he and Moore put together a small group of musicians who could double on instruments and create a bigger sound. Billy Jack Wills and His Western Swing Band never numbered more than seven members, but with a daily broadcast over KFBK and a signal directed toward the Northwest, they soon became the hottest band in the northwestern states.

By 1954, television changed the entertainment habits across the United States, and dance bands suffered. Bob had to close down in Texas and take over Billy Jack's band. It was not long before they closed the dance hall, and Billy Jack tried unsuccessfully to make a musical living in other areas. He moved to Shawnee, Oklahoma, and worked as a plumber. On March 2, 1991, he died and was buried in Tulsa alongside his family.

# LUTHER JAY "LUKE" WILLS

*Born near Memphis, Texas, September 10, 1920*

The third son born to John and Emma Wills, Luke Wills became the bass player as well as a guitar player. In 1936, Bob Wills bought his parents a farm near Muleshoe, Texas, but John wanted to try his hand with a radio band. He and his sixteen-year-old son, Luke, started playing over KICA in Clovis, New Mexico, as well as appearances on other stations in the region. This schedule kept Luke away from school and John away from farm work. Within two years they had to return to Tulsa.

**Luke Wills. (Photograph courtesy of Lorene Wills.)**

In Tulsa, Luke played bass in Johnnie Lee's first band, and in 1940, John, Johnnie Lee, and Luke moved to Fort Smith, Arkansas, to work that radio/dance market. In a short time, they were back in Tulsa where Johnnie Lee hired members from the Alabama Boys and started a band that lasted for twenty-five years; Luke played bass in that band.

Wills went into the navy during World War II, and after he was discharged, he joined Bob in California. The demand for Bob Wills and the Texas Playboys was so great that Bob made Luke put together a band in Fresno to play the dances in that region. Known as Luke Wills' Rhythm Busters, they recorded a few sides for King Records before Luke rejoined Bob and the Playboys.

Through the 1950s, Luke played bass for Bob, and in 1960 moved to Las Vegas where he lives in retirement.

## SWIFT'S JEWEL COWBOYS

*Birth information not found*

In the early 1930s, it was common practice for grocery producers to sponsor bands to advertise their goods, so in 1933, the manager of the Houston, Texas, Swift and Company's Jewel Salad Oil and Jewel Shortening refinery, Frank B. Collins, decided that a cowboy band could sell their products. He organized the Jewel Cowboys on April 8, 1933, but shortly after, Collins was transferred to Memphis, Tennessee. He organized a new group that grew to seven members and operated out of Memphis.

The band played dances, stage shows, rodeos, county fairs, and radio shows, eventually being featured on CBS Radio. They advertised that they were the only mounted cowboy band—each member owned his own horse and rigging. Of course, this advertising gimmick resulted in broken bones and other problems because they were not good horsemen. Their recordings—only "Chuck Wagon Swing" and "My Untrue Cowgirl" even came close to being western—were issued on Vocalion and Okeh labels. They disbanded during World War II.

Leon Rausch. (Photograph courtesy of Leon Rausch.)

## LEON RAUSCH

*Born in Springfield, Missouri, October 2, 1927*

Born into a musical family, Rausch grew up playing and singing country music, but after service in the navy during World War II, he expanded his musical horizons into western swing.

Rausch moved to Tulsa in 1955 and worked for Bob Wills as well as being a member of the Johnnie Lee Wills band until 1964. Then he moved to Fort Worth and organized the New Texas Playboys, becoming a member of the Original Texas Playboys headed by Leon McAuliffe in 1976. He has received numerous awards for being the major singer perpetuating the western swing singing style. Rausch continues to appear with the Texas Playboys and is the featured vocalist on numerous western swing recordings.

**Light Crust Doughboys in Fort Worth, Texas, 1932. From left to right— Milton Brown, Durwood Brown, Truitt Kimzey (announcer), Bob Wills, and Herman Arnspiger. (Guy Logsdon and the Ranch House Library.)**

# LIGHT CRUST DOUGHBOYS

*Birth information not found*

The Light Crust Doughboys hold the longevity record in western swing music, even though they were not always a dance band. Bob Wills, Milton Brown, and Herman Arnspiger worked as the Alladin Laddies until they were sponsored by Burrus Mills and Light Crust Flour, broadcasting over KFJZ, Fort Worth. They were the original Light Crust Doughboys. Brown left in 1932, and Wills left in 1933, but Arnspiger stayed with the band until Wills hired him to be a Texas Playboy. Leon McAuliffe and other well-known names in western swing became members before moving on to larger and better-known bands or becoming bandleaders. Even Hank Thompson and His Brazos Valley Boys broadcast under the sponsorship of Light Crust Flour.

Through the years, different bandleaders and bands used the name with the latest group recording and appearing under the leadership of Art Greenhaw and Smoky Montgomery.

# WILLIAM LEMUEL "BILL" BOYD

*Born in Fannin County, Texas, September 29, 1910*

Boyd grew up hearing his parents sing old ballads. He purchased a mail-order guitar and as a teenager decided that a music career was better than life on the farm. In 1929, the family moved to Dallas, where Boyd and his brother, Jim, met Art Davis. Soon they were playing music for students in Dallas Tech High School, and Bill, with two other friends, eventually landed a show on WFAA, Dallas, as "Alexander's Daybreakers."

In 1932, Boyd organized the Cowboy Ramblers for a show on WRR and on August 7, 1934, in San Antonio, recorded western string-band songs under the name Bill Boyd and His Cowboy Ramblers for Victor Records. The original members were Bill Boyd, guitar; Jim Boyd, bass; Art Davis, fiddle; and Walter Kirkes, banjo. Boyd's music is usually referred to as western swing; however, western string is more appropriate, for they rarely played dances. Patrons did dance to their recordings on juke boxes in bars and cafes.

Boyd's band was a radio performance and recording group, and the band grew in size as their popularity grew. Boyd used excellent musicians who came from or went to larger western swing organizations such as swing fiddlers Cecil Brower and Jesse Ashlock, and piano man Knocky Parker. For his recording sessions in 1937 and 1938, he had a ten-piece band.

In the early 1940s, Boyd went to Hollywood and starred in six B-westerns for Producers Releasing Corporation, and he continued recording for Victor until 1950. Bill Boyd died in 1977.

Bill Boyd and His Cowboy Ramblers. From left to right—Jim Boyd, Jake Wright, Billie Jack Saucier, Bill Boyd (at mike), Clyde Boyd, Cleo Hoyt, Freddy Casares, and Bill Osborne. (Guy Logsdon and the Ranch House Library.)

# ADOLPH HOFNER

*Birth information not found*

Adolph Hofner was born in the south central part of Texas that is populated by German and Czech descendants and dominated by a love of polka music. He became a guitar player/vocalist, while his brother Emil learned the steel guitar.

In 1936, the Hofner brothers joined Jimmy Revard's Oklahoma Playboys, and when Revard left, Hofner returned to San Antonio as leader of the group. He changed the name to Adolph Hofner and His Texans, and in World War II on the West Coast, he was Dolph Hofner and his San Antonians.

After the war, Hofner returned to San Antonio and mixed his polka tunes with western swing, earning a loyal following in the region. The band was sponsored by Pearl Beer, and three decades later, the member's shirts still had Pearl Beer stenciled across the backs. He always employed veteran musicians and played the crowd-pleasing music his fans requested most.

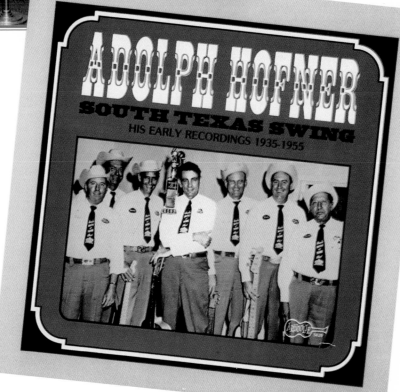

Adolph Hofner on the cover of *South Texas Swing: His Early Recordings 1935–1955*, Arhoolie Productions, 1980.

## PFEIFFER BROTHERS

*Born Wiley Jim Pfeiffer in Mansfield, Ohio, December 12, 1955 and David Earl Pfeiffer in Mansfield, Ohio, November 11, 1963*

The Pfeiffer Brothers play a western swing style of cowboy/western music with genuine sibling harmonies and a tight instrumental sound. They specialize in the western and western swing repertoire of such early artists as Milton Brown and Sons of the Pioneers. Jim started on fiddle but switched to guitar, and David Earl settled on bass. Located in Salida, Colorado, since 1992, the two brothers have been performing at many cowboy/western gatherings and festivals as well as on the guest-ranch circuit. Their first release as a duo was *Wah-Hoo!* (WP, 1993).

## LAURA LEE (OWENS) MCBRIDE

*Born in Bridgeport, Oklahoma, May 16, 1920*

The first child born to Tex and Maude Owens, Laura Lee and her younger sister, Jane, performed on radio and stage with their father, using the names Joy and Jane. When Laura grew older, she dropped her middle name, Francis, and started using Lee.

After earning a reputation for her singing and yodeling, she was hired by Bob Wills in 1943 and became the first female singer in the Playboys organization. When she left Wills, she joined Tex Ritter, and during her career, she performed on most western music radio and television shows. Her husband was western musician/singer Dickie McBride. She died January 25, 1989.

## AUBREY "MOON" MULLICAN

*Born in Polk County, Texas, March 29, 1909*

At an early age, Mullican developed a style of playing the piano with two fingers in the upper register, supported by a solid left-hand bass. His style influenced numerous country musicians but had limited influence in the jazz styles heard in western bands. He worked in Texas bands, specifically with Cliff Bruner's Texas Wanderers, and he sang with such a distinctive style that he became a popular solo performer and King Records-recording star with songs such as "I'll Sail My Ship Alone." Mullican was a mixture of many musical forms—Eastern, Western, Cajun, and Mullican. He died in Beaumont, Texas, January 1, 1967.

**The Pfeiffer Brothers. (*Song of the West* collection.)**

**Home Town Jamboree, Cliffe Stone, leader. (Guy Logsdon and the Ranch House Library.)**

# CLIFFIE STONE
## (CLIFFORD GILPIN SNYDER)

*Born in Burbank, California, March 1, 1917*

Cliffie Stone grew up in an atmosphere of western music. His father was musician/comedian Herman the Hermit, and while a young man Stone worked as an early radio disc jockey on stations such as KFVD, Hollywood. He was a session bass-fiddle player on numerous West Coast recordings and became a recording executive with Capitol Records.

Stone led the popular radio/television/dance show "Hometown Jamboree," and worked with Merle Travis on hits such as "Divorce Me C.O.D.," "No Vacancy," and "So Round, So Firm, So Fully Packed." He also helped develop the careers of stars such as Tennessee Ernie Ford. In recent years, he has headed the Gene Autry music production division, continuing to live in his native state.

SMOKE! SMOKE! SMOKE!
(THAT CIGARETTE)

Words and Music by
MERLE TRAVIS and TEX WILLIAMS

Featured by MERLE TRAVIS
Star of Capitol Records and Columbia Broadcasting System

AMERICAN MUSIC, INC.
9109 Sunset Blvd., Hollywood, Calif.

**Merle Travis on the cover of "Smoke! Smoke! Smoke! (That Cigarette)," American Music, Inc., 1947. (Guy Logsdon and the Ranch House Library.)**

## MERLE TRAVIS

*Born in Rosewood, Kentucky, November 29, 1917*

This legendary guitarist, singer, and songwriter gained his fame after World War II, working and recording with western artists and bands in the Los Angeles area. He perfected the finger-picking guitar style and was a major influence on Chet Atkins, Hank Thompson, and probably millions of professional and amateur guitarists. As guitarist on thousands of West Coast recordings, he worked with Cliffe Stone, Ray Whitley, Jimmy Wakely, Tex Ritter, and many other western stars.

Travis's songs, "Divorce Me C.O.D." and "Smoke, Smoke, Smoke That Cigarette," saved Capitol Records from financial failure, and other songs have become traditional in American music. Travis died in his home in Tahlequah, Oklahoma, October 20, 1983.

## CRAIG CHAMBERS

*Born in Houston, Texas, January 30, 1945*

Chambers wrote and scored the music and narrated the Broadway production *The Best Little Whorehouse in Texas*. He is a guitarist, singer, and songwriter who, as a member of the Time-Warp Tophands, recorded the five-volume *How the West Was Swung*. He organized and led the original Rio Grande Band and is heard on *Playin' for the Door*. Also a horseman, Chambers lives in California, where he trains horses and continues to record.

## BILLY JOE PARKER

*Born in Tuskegee, Oklahoma, July 19, 1937*

This award-winning disc jockey is heard throughout the West over KVOO Radio, Tulsa, Oklahoma. He and John Wooley, entertainment writer for the *Tulsa World*, host "Wooley Wednesday," a weekly radio show that features western swing. It is rebroadcast each Wednesday evening with KVOO beamed to reach all western states. In the 1970s, Parker traveled with Ernest Tubb as a country/western vocalist and has recorded several albums including his own songs.

## GEORGE STRAIT

*Born in Poteet, Texas, May 18, 1952*

George Strait was raised on a ranch in Texas. After attending college for a brief spell, he eloped with his high school sweetheart, Norma, and joined the army. While in the service, Strait formed country bands, focusing on the influences of Merle Haggard, Bob Wills, Hank Williams, and George Jones, among others. Returning to college after his discharge, he played in bands at night and attended classes by day. He was soon signed by the MCA label because of his strong west Texas following. After starting his professional career in 1981, the country chart toppers soon followed.

Strait is heralded as a return to "old time country," and readily admits that his Ace in the Hole band is patterned after Bob Wills's Texas Playboys. He has even performed with members of the Playboys on television and has recorded a few tunes from the songbook of Bob Wills.

# ELDON SHAMBLIN

*Born in Weatherford, Oklahoma, April 24, 1916*

Eldon Shamblin is the world's greatest and most influential rhythm guitarist. He created the sound that is often called Texas Swing Guitar but should be known as Tulsa Swing; his rhythm guitar sounds are heard throughout the western states and often in Nashville recording sessions.

Shamblin is a self-taught guitarist, who in the early years of the Great Depression moved to Oklahoma City to earn food and meager subsistence with his singing and guitar. He worked the Oklahoma City bars for food and tips, until 1935 when he met a group of musicians who became the original Alabama Boys in Tulsa. They hired Shamblin as their vocalist, but since he did not like to sing, he worked at perfecting a distinctive guitar sound.

In November 1937, Bob Wills talked Shamblin into becoming a Texas Playboy, and while recording "Take Me Back to Tulsa" in 1941, Wills turned to Shamblin and said, "I want you to put a lot of runs in this." From that time on, Shamblin played a strong running bass line sustained by inverted substitute, passing chord structures—a constantly moving rhythm voice. And, he is equally innovative when playing lead guitar.

Eldon Shamblin, "World's Greatest Rhythm Guitarist," playing the Fender Stratocaster given to him by Leo Fender, believed to be the prototype of his famous guitar model, at Cain's Ballroom in Tulsa, Oklahoma, 1979. Bob Wills's photograph is behind him. (Photograph by Guy Logsdon.)

Shamblin and Leon McAuliffe developed steel guitar/standard guitar duets that became classic guitar sounds, and it was after Shamblin joined the Playboys that the heavy rhythm, Wills's musical trademark, became obvious in their recordings. He arranged songs for the band and eventually became the friend who looked after Bob Wills.

After the big western-swing-band era ended, he worked for Hoyle Nix in Big Springs, Texas, before returning to Tulsa, where he tuned pianos for his primary living. In the 1970s and 1980s, he toured and recorded with Merle Haggard and was a member of the Original Texas Playboys. In recent years, he has recorded with younger musicians such as Mark O'Conner, and he continues to work with the various Texas Playboy bands. Eldon Shamblin was most recently heard on the 1993 Grammy-winner "Red Wing" with Asleep at the Wheel. He lives in Tulsa.

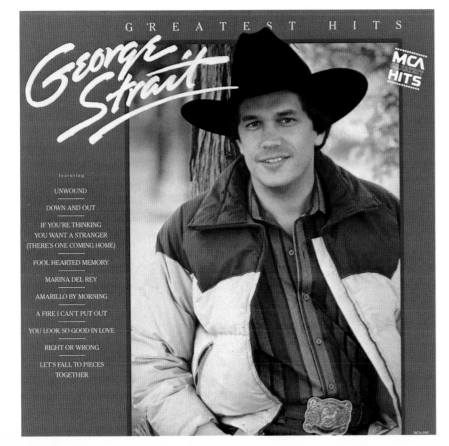

George Strait cover for his *Greatest Hits* CD, MCA Records, 1985. (*Song of the West* collection.)

# Sons of the West

*Birth information not found*

In 1936, Bob Wills and the Texas Playboys received far more requests for dance engagements than they could accept; many were farther than the band could drive in time to play the dance and return to Tulsa for their KVOO broadcast. Bob's cousin, Son Lansford, was the Playboy bass player, so Bob decided to send him to Amarillo with a band to play engagements that the Playboys could not work. Bob provided the money to hire the band and to get established at the Rainbow Gardens Dance Hall under the name, Sons of the West; however, Lansford was not a leader, and he soon returned to Tulsa. Jimmie Meek assumed the leader's role. They broadcast over KGNC and in September 1938 recorded ten sides for Decca Records. Steel guitar player Billy Briggs was the dominant figure in this band, who remained popular in west Texas until World War II stopped their music.

# Asleep at the Wheel

*Ray Benson (lead vocals, guitar), born in Philadelphia, Pennsylvania, March 16, 1951. (Member of earlier editions of this group have included Leroy Preston (vocals, guitar), Lucky Oceans (pseudonym for Reuben Gosfield); (pedal steel guitar), Chris O'Connell (female vocals), and Floyd Domino (piano). More recent members have included Ricky Turpin (fiddle), Tim Alexander (piano, accordion), Michael Francis (saxophone), Cindy Cashdollar (steel guitar), David Miller (bass), and Tommy Beaver (drums).*

A contemporary western swing-oriented group, Asleep at the Wheel's one constant member has been singer/guitarist Ray Benson. They began as a country band in Paw Paw, West Virginia. Finding the blues, swing and improvisation, and all aspects of western swing music appealing, their sound moved in that direction. Inspired by Merle Haggard's album *Tribute to the Best Damn Fiddle Player in the World (Or My Salute to Bob Wills)*, the group moved to Oakland to play to receptive *western* audiences. Eventually, they settled in Austin, Texas.

In 1977, Asleep at the Wheel were voted "Top Touring Band" by the Academy of Country Music, along with the Sons of the Pioneers, and they received Grammies for their renditions of Count Basie's "One O'Clock Jump" (1978), "String of Pearls" (1987), and "Sugarfoot Rag" (1988). Several of their hits appear on the budget-priced *Swing Time* (Sony, 1992). Their *Tribute to Bob Wills and the Texas Playboys* (Liberty, 1993,) featured such western swing greats as Johnny Gimble, Leon Rausch, Herb Remington, Eldon Shamblin, and George Strait, as well as a number of popular country singers.

Besides finding a cowboy/western act booked at a county or state fair or at a folk, bluegrass, or country music festival, quality cowboy/western acts can be heard regularly at a few spots. Cowboy and western music doesn't have a geographical center, unlike country which is based in Nashville. Cowboy artists tend to be individualistic loners with a strong tradition of D.I.Y. (do it yourself). Lobby organizations haven't united musicians nor has public demand spurred profitable touring circuits for artists. Most western acts do their own public relations and generate their own mailing lists to keep their fans apprised of where they will be performing.

Please note: At tourist areas throughout the western states, many operations provide western-style musical entertainment and dinner for a single price. The caliber of these places run from good to embarrassing. For the uninitiated who have never experienced western music, they might be a welcome introduction. These establishments usually hire performers who have no involvement with the art of cowboy and western music other than using it as a means of steady employment. Be fore-warned.

## JANUARY
### Cowboy Poetry Gathering
Elko, Nevada, always the last weekend in January

This is the premier cowboy poetry gathering in the United States, and it's also the best place to hear great cowboy and western music. Because this event attracts the finest in artists and the most devoted of fans, every year those in attendance are assured of great programs and (even better in our eyes) an exceptional environment to socialize. The great musicians come in the dead of winter, paid or not, the calling is so strong! Open sessions at Elko underline their policy on allowing performers access to showcase their music, and many a cowboy has started a career offstage at Elko.
Contact:
The Western Folklife Center
P.O. Box 888
501 Railroad Street
Elko, NV 89802
(702) 738-7508

## APRIL
### Cowboy Songs and Range Ballads
Cody, Wyoming, first weekend in April

The oldest yearly festival mentioned here, this intimate music gathering emphasizes the music of ranch cowboys and their folk arts.
Contact:
The Buffalo Bill Historical Center
P.O. Box 1000
Cody, WY 82414
(307) 587-4771

## JUNE
### WestFest
New Mexico, mid June

Michael Martin Murphey's western multi-cultural event held in his home state of New Mexico.
Contact:
Littlehorn Communications
Bridget Dolan Little
3108 Stoneybrook Road
Oklahoma City, OK 73120
(405) 755-8288

## Cowboy Music Gathering
Elko, Nevada, mid June

Another event run by The Western Folklife folks. Emphasis is on music by people with ranching traditions.
Contact:
The Western Folklife Center
P.O. Box 888
501 Railroad Street
Elko, NV 89802
(702) 738-7508

## SEPTEMBER
### Michael Martin Murphey's WestFest
Copper Mountain Resort, Colorado, Labor Day weekend

The largest of all, this festival is held in the Rocky Mountains of Colorado. Expect all things from western to cowboy to Indian to commercial country music.
Contact:
Copper Mountain Resort or
Littlehorn Communications
Bridget Dolan Little
3108 Stoneybrook Road
Oklahoma City, OK 73120
(405) 755-8288

## OCTOBER
### Lincoln County Cowboy Symposium
Ruidoso, New Mexico, October

This symposium is held at the Ruidoso Super Select Sales Pavilion and is full of cowboy and western swing music, spearheaded by Ray Reed.
Contact:
Lincoln County Cowboy Symposium
P.O. Box 1679
Ruidoso Downs, NM 88346
(505) 378-4142

### Red Steagall Cowboy Gathering & Swing Festival
Fort Worth Stockyards, Texas, October

This gathering is becoming a must for lovers of Texas western swing.
Contact:
The Texas Agricultural Extension Service

500 Jones Ave.
Fort Worth, TX 76102

## NOVEMBER
### Western Music Festival
Tucson, Arizona, November.

The Western Music Association sponsors this yearly event. The shows predominately feature the Western Music Association's own members, some of whom are the country's favorite western performers.
Contact:
Western Music Association
3900 E. Nimrod
Tucson, AZ 85711
(602) 323-3311

## ON-GOING ALL SUMMER:
### The Home Ranch
World-class resort owned by western music patron Cowboy Ken Jones.

Besides offering exceptional ranch vacations and gourmet food, Ken makes sure his guests are introduced to cowboy and western music by either the Rockin' U Wranglers or a Home Ranch invited guest musician.
Contact:
The Home Ranch
P. O. Box 822
Clark, CO 80428
(303) 879-1780

## During Tourist Seasons:
The Chuckwagons of the West Organizations operate "Chuckwagons," a dinner and comedy music show. Quality varies from location to location, but you can count on a family-oriented (if somewhat corny) show. The music covers popular western songs of the past, sometimes mixed with crowd-pleasing country and bluegrass material. These businesses are committed to bringing you a good time on your vacation (call beforehand as most of these operations are seasonal and often are sold out).
Triple C Chuckwagon
8900 W. Bopp Rd.
Tucson, AZ 85746
(602) 883-2333

Rockin' R Chuckwagon
6136 E. Baseline Rd.
Mesa, AZ 85206
(602) 832-1539

Flying J Chuckwagon
P.O. Box 2505
Ruidoso, NM 88345
(505) 336-4330

Bar D Chuckwagon
8080 County Road 250
Durango, CO 81301
(303) 247-5753

Flying W Chuckwagon
3330 Chuckwagon Rd.
Colorado Springs, CO 80919
(719) 598-4000

Lazy B Chuckwagon
1915 Dry Gulch Rd.
Estes Park, CO 80517
(303) 586-5371

Bar J Chuckwagon
P.O. Box 220
Wilson, WY 83014
(307) 733-5386

Circle B Chuckwagon
HC33 Box 3611
Rapid City, SD 57701
(605) 348-7358

# Some Trusty Sources for Recorded Cowboy and Western Music

**Cowboy Country General Store**
P.O. Box 1464
Laporte, CO 80535
(303) 482-5960

**Gene Autry Western Heritage Museum**
Museum Store
4700 Western Heritage Way
Los Angeles, CA 90027-1462
(213) 667-2000, ext. 288

**Frontier Records**
P.O. Box 157
Jenks, OK 74037
(918) 745-2152

**Ranch House Library**
P.O. Box 520982
Tulsa, OK 74152
(918) 743-2171

**Roots & Rhythm**
6921 Stockton Ave.
El Cerrito, CA 94530
(510) 525-1494

**Roundup Records**
One Camp Street
Cambridge, MA 02140-1194
(617) 661-6306

***Song of the West***
The Magazine of Cowboy & Western Music
136 Pearl St.
Fort Collins, CO 80521-2424
(303) 484-3209

**Western Folklife Center**
Store & Cowboy Shopping List
P.O. Box 888
501 Railroad Street
Elko, NV 8903
(702) 738-7508

# A Selected Discography of Cowboy and Western Music

The following discography constitutes a basic library of cowboy and western music, historical, and contemporary. Most of them, but not all, are available in the compact-disc and cassette-tape formats.

## Gene Autry:

*The Essential Gene Autry* (1933–1946) (Columbia/Legacy)
*The Gene Autry Columbia Historic Edition* (Columbia)
These two albums provide a good sampling of America's first popular singing cowboy.

## Don Edwards:

*Desert Nights and Cowtown Blues* (SevenShoux)
*Chant of the Wanderer* (SevenShoux)
*Songs of the Trail* (Warner Western)
*Goin' Back to Texas* (Warner Western)
On these four albums a variety of cowboy, western, and western swing songs are performed by one of cowboy/western's finest voices.

## Ramblin' Jack Elliott:

*Hard Travelin'* (Fantasy)
*The Essential Ramblin' Jack Elliott* (Vanguard)
These two albums are a fine example of cowboy folk music as sung by the idiosyncratic Ramblin' Jack.

## Harry Jackson:

*The Cowboy: His Songs, Ballads and Brag Talk* (Smithsonian Folkways)
One of a few cowboy folk singers who holds true to the original form, Harry Jackson performs cowboy ballads a capella.

## Katie Lee

*Colorado River Songs* (Katydid Records)
*Fenced!* (Katydid Records)
*Ten Thousand Goddam Cattle* (Katydid Records)
Katie Lee is a lady folksinger who sings of the changing West with the fire, grace, and wit of few cowboy balladeers.

## John McEuen

*The Wild West* (Mogull Entertainment)
Originally a soundtrack for a television miniseries, this landmark album collects 45 tracks and is 79 minutes in length, featuring artists such as Don Edwards, Red Steagall, Bill Miller, Colcannon, Michael Martin Murphey, Marty Stuart, Crystal Gayle, and many others, singing and playing the music of the historic West.

## Gary McMahan:

*Saddle 'Em Up and Go!* (Horseapple Records)
A true Westerner, McMahan is a classic contemporary cowboy singer/songwriter.

## Bill Miller:

*The Red Road* (Warner Western)
American Indian poet/storyteller/singer/songwriter/guitarist Miller delivers a haunting, personal set on *The Red Road.*

## Michael Martin Murphey:

*Cowboy Songs* (Warner Bros.)
*Cowboy Songs II: Cowboy Christmas* (Warner Bros.)
*Cowboy Songs III: Rhymes of the Renegades* (Warner Western)
Singer/songwriter/guitarist Murphey delivers an entertaining experience on all of these—especially the Christmas album.

## Buck Ramsey:

*Rolling Uphill from Texas*
Few can sing and emote the old cowboy songs as Buck Ramsey can.

## Riders in the Sky:

*Three on the Trail* (Rounder)
*Cowboy Jubilee* (Rounder)
*Prairie Serenade* (Rounder)
*Saddle Pals* (Rounder)
*The Cowboy Way* (MCA)
*Horse Opera* (MCA)
Of their many albums, these five demonstrate the finest Riders in the Sky singing, clowning, and tune playing.

**Tex Ritter:**
*High Noon* (Bear Family)
*Lady Killin' Cowboy* (Bear Family)
*Singin' in the Saddle* (Bear Family)
The late Tex Ritter's lovable voice is a real pleasure to hear, as these albums will attest.

**Marty Robbins:**
*Gunfighter Ballads and Trail Songs* (Columbia)
*More Gunfighter Ballads and Trail Songs* (Columbia)
Although he wrote and sang in a number of formats, these two albums showcase Robbins' beautiful western balladry.

**Roy Rogers:**
*Roll On Texas Moon* (Bear Family)
*The Roy Rogers Columbia Historic Edition* (Columbia)
Roy Rogers's likable western singing voice is well served by these two anthologies.

**Tom Russell:**
*Cowboy Real* (Philo)
This is a haunting original cowboy folk album of the highest order.

**Sons of the Pioneers:**
*Sons of the Pioneers* (Country Music Hall of Fame Series MCA)
*Sons of the Pioneers* (Columbia Historic Edition)
*Tumbling Tumbleweeds—The RCA Victor Years, Vol. 1* (RCA)
or *Wagons West* (Bear Family)
The Sons of the Pioneers created the western harmony sound. Each album is from a different era. Their era with the most hits (RCA) is best represented by the CD/cassette *Tumbling Tumbleweeds* or, for the most complete, the four-CD set *Wagons West*.

**Sons of the San Joaquin:**
*Songs of the Silver Screen* (Warner Western)
This album demonstrates the Sons of the San Joaquin's considerable vocal prowess.

**Sourdough Slim:**
*Half Baked*
Sourdough Slim really shines on this goofy, fun-loving album.

**Red Steagall:**
*Born to this Land* (Warner Western)
Red Steagall showcases his strong writing (poetry and song) and vocal skills on *Born to this Land*.

**Ian Tyson:**
*Old Corrals & Sagebrush* (Stony Plain)
*Ian Tyson* (Stony Plain)
*Cowboyography* (Stony Plain)
*I Outgrew the Wagon* (Stony Plain)
*And Stood There Amazed* (Stony Plain)
*Eighteen Inches of Rain* (Stony Plain)
Ian Tyson has written, recorded, and released an impressive body of work. Many of the songs herein are cowboy love songs, realistically written by the master. His *Cowboyography* remains a hugely popular work.

**Bob Wills and His Texas Playboys:**
*Anthology (1935-1973)* (Rhino)
*The Tiffany Transcriptions, Vol. 4, You're From Texas* (Rhino)
The late Bob Wills remains a popular (and influential) figure of western swing. *Anthology (1935–1973)* is a good introduction to the different eras of Wills's work; the Tiffany collection is a free-swinging set of Texas songs by the Playboys.

**Anthology Albums:**
*Cowboy Songs on Folkways* (Smithsonian Folkways)
A great introduction to some of Smithsonian Folkways' great collection. Includes Leadbelly, Woody Guthrie, Harry Jackson, Cisco Houston, and others.
*Back In the Saddle Again—American Cowboy Songs* (New World Records)
This impressive anthology runs the gamut from Haywire Mac's "The Old Chisholm Trail" to Riders in the Sky's "Cowboy Song" in its twenty-eight selections.
*Okeh Western Swing* (Columbia Special Products)
This anthology is an excellent sample of early swing and string bands.
*Song of the West* (Rhino)
This four-CD, seventy-three-track volume includes everything from the Pioneers' "Tumbling Tumbleweeds" to Slim Pickens's version of "Desperados Waiting for a Train."

# STATE SONGS

### Arizona
An Arizona Home
Arizona Days
Ridin' North of the Arizona Moon
Arizona Sunset
Arizona Waltz
Going Back to Arizona
Dear Old Arizona Home
Old Arizona
Sedona, Arizona
The Sierry Petes

### California
California
High Sierra
Out California Way
Out in Pioneertown
Sierra Nevada
San Fernando Valley
Song of the Sierras

### Colorado
Colorado
Colorado Bound
Colorado Blue
Colorado Home
Colorado Sunset
Colorado Waltz
I Want to Follow the Swallow Back to Colorado

### Dakotas
The Dakota Land
The Dreary Black Hills

### Idaho
Idaho Winds
Idaho Moon
On the Trail to Idaho
Springtime Comes Late to Idaho
(Way Beyond the Hills of) Idaho
Way Out in Idaho

### Kansas
In Kansas
The Kansas Line
Wichita
Way Out West in Kansas

### Montana
Blue Montana Skies
Hills of Old Montana
Montana Moon
Montana
Montana Rodeo
Montana Waltz
My Home's in Montana
Take Me Back to Old Montana

### Nevada
Big Time In Elko
Over Nevada
Nevada
Old Nevada Moon
When It's Nighttime in Nevada
When It's Roundup Time in Reno

### New Mexico
A-L-B-U-Q-U-E-R-Q-U-E
I'm Going to Gallop, Gallop to Gallop, New Mexico
Land of Enchantment
Lights of Old Santa Fe
Lonesome New Mexico Wind
Old Dolores
Riding Down to Santa Fe
Ridin' Down the Trail to Albuquerque
Santa Fe, New Mexico
South of Santa Fe

### Oklahoma
All Aboard for Oklahoma
For Oklahoma, I'm Yearning
Good Ole Oklahoma
Home In Oklahoma
My Oklahoma Home
My Oklahoma
Oklahoma's Calling
Oklahoma Gals
Oklahoma Hills
Oklahoma Rag
Oklahoma Stomp
Oklahoma Twister
O.K. Oklahoma
Okie Boogie
Sweet Home In Oklahoma
Take Me Back to Tulsa
The Cherokee Strip

The Everlasting Hills of Oklahoma
Tulsa Stomp
T-U-L-S-A Straight Ahead
Tulsa Waltz

## *Texas*
Across the Alley from the Alamo
Aha, San Antone
Beautiful Texas
Blue Bonnet Lane
Blue Bonnet Rag
Boggy Road to Texas
Can't Get Enough of Texas
Can't Get Texas Out of Me
Can't Shake the Sands of Texas From My Shoes
Deep in the Heart of Texas
El Paso
El Paso City
Even Texas Isn't Big Enough Now
Fort Worth Stomp
Full Moon Over Texas
Going Back to Texas
Headin' for Texas and Home
Home in San Antone
Hop, Skip and Jump Over Texas
I'd Like to be in Texas When They Roundup in the Spring
I'll Go Ridin' Down That Old Texas Trail
I'm Going to Leave Old Texas Now
Little Ol' State of Texas
Lone Star Rag
Next to the X in Texas
Old El Paso
Old Texas
Rainbow Over Texas
Roll On, Texas Moon
Starlighting Time in Texas
San Angelo
San Antonio Rose
South Texas Swing
Texas Blues
Texas Crapshooter
Texas Double Eagle
Texas Drummer Boy
Texas Fiddler
Texas Hambone Blues
Texas Hills
Texas Home

Texas Polka
Texas Plains
Texas Sand
Texas Skiparoo
Texas Star
Texas Stomp
Texas Tornado
Texas Trails
Texas Two Step
Texas Waltz
T for Texas
The Eyes of Texas
The Texan Boys
The Texas Cowboy
The Texas Rangers
The Texas Trail
Trail to Old San Antone
Underneath A Wide West Texas Sky
Under Stars Over Texas
Waltz Across Texas
Waltzing in Old San Antone
Way Out West in Texas
West Texas Highway
West Texas Cowboy
You Can't Get The Hell in Texas
You're From Texas

## *Utah*
The Red Hills of Utah
Utah Trail

## *Wyoming*
Home Again in Ol' Wyoming
Home in Old Wyoming
Lights of Laramie
Old Cheyenne
Someday in Wyoming
Somewhere in Old Wyoming
Song of Wyoming
Sweet Wyoming Home
The Hills of Old Wyomin'
Wendin' My Way to Wyoming

Guy Logsdon is an internationally recognized authority on western and cowboy music, poetry, and musicians. He is the author of the award-winning *"The Whorehouse Bells Were Ringing" and Other Songs Cowboys Sing* and numerous other writings about the American West. He also compiled *Cowboy Songs on Folkways* for Smithsonian/Folkways, one of the most important cowboy song anthologies ever produced.

Mary Rogers and William Jacobson are publishers of *Song of the West: The Magazine of Cowboy and Western Music*. Jacobson is known as an authority on cowboy and western music and has had articles published in *Option* and *Cowboy Magazine*. Rogers is an ardent supporter of modern cowboy and western songwriters, because she feels this is a living, evolving musical form.